1. Introduction

Complex issues arise in spatial analysis, many of which are neither clearly defined nor completely resolved, but form the basis for current research. The most fundamental of these is the problem of defining the spatial location of the entities being studied. For example, a study on human health could describe the spatial position of humans with a point placed where they live, or with a point located where they work, or by using a line to describe their weekly trips; each choice has dramatic effects on the techniques which can be used for the analysis and on the conclusions which can be obtained. Other issues in spatial analysis include the limitations of mathematical knowledge, the assumptions required by existing statistical techniques, and problems in computer based calculations.

Classification of the techniques of spatial analysis is difficult because of the large number of different fields of research involved, the different fundamental approaches which can be chosen, and the many forms the data can take.

Geographic analysis allows us to study and understand the real world processes by developing and applying manipulation, analysis criteria and models and to carryout integrated modeling . These criteria illuminate underlying trends in geographic data, making new information available. A GIS enhances this process by providing tools, which can be combined in meaningful sequence to reveal new or previously unidentified relationships within or between data sets, thus increasing better understanding of real world. The results of geographic analysis can be commercial in the form of maps, reports or both. Integration involves bringing together diverse information from a variety of sources and analysis of multi-parameter data to provide answers and solutions to defined problems.

Spatial analysis is the vital part of GIS. It can be done in two ways. One is the vector-based and the other is raster-based analysis. Since the advent of GIS in the 1980s, many government agencies have invested heavily in GIS installations, including   the purchase   of hardware and software and the construction of mammoth databases. Two fundamental functions of GIS have been widely realized: generation of maps and generation of tabular reports.

Indeed, GIS provides a very effective tool for generating maps and statistical reports from a database.   However, GIS functionality far exceeds the purposes of mapping and report compilation. In addition to the basic functions related to automated cartography and data base management systems, the most important uses of GIS are spatial analysis capabilities. As spatial information is organized in a GIS, it should be able to answer complex questions regarding space. Making maps alone does not justify the high cost of building a GIS. The same maps may be produced using a simpler cartographic package. Likewise, if the purpose   is to generate tabular output, then a simpler database management system or a statistical package may be a more efficient solution. It is spatial analysis that requires the logical connections between attribute data and map features, and the operational procedures built on the spatial relationships among map features. These capabilities make GIS a much more powerful   and cost-effective tool than automated cartographic packages, statistical packages, or data base management systems. Indeed, functions required for performing spatial analyses that are

1

not available in either cartographic packages or database management systems are commonly implemented in GIS.

What is Special about Spatial Data?

An attention to location, spatial interaction, spatial structure and spatial processes lies at the heart of research in several subdisciplines in the social sciences. Empirical studies in these fields routinely employ data for which locational attributes (the "where") are an important source of information. Such data typically consist of one or a few crosssections of observations for either micro-units, such as households, store sites, settlements, or for aggregate spatial units, such as electoral districts, counties, states or even countries. Observations such as these, for which the absolute location and/or relative positioning (spatial arrangement) is taken into account are referred to as spatial data. In the social sciences, they have been utilized in a wide range of studies, such as archeological investigations of ancient settlement patterns (e.g., in Whitley and Clark, 1985, and Kvamme, 1990), sociological and anthropological studies of social networks (e.g., in White et al., 1981, and Doreian et al., 1984), demographic analyses of geographical trends in mortality and fertility (e.g., in Cook and Pocock, 1983, and Loftin and Ward, 1983), and political models of spatial patterns in international conflict and cooperation (e.g., in O'Loughlin, 1985, and O'Loughlin and Anselin, 1991). Furthermore, in urban and regional economics and regional science, spatial data are at the core of the field and are studied to model the spatial structure for a range of socioeconomic variables, such as unemployment rates (Bronars and Jansen, 1987), household consumer demand (Case, 1991), and prices for gasoline (Haining, 1984) or housing (Dubin, 1992).

The locational attributes of spatial data (i.e., for the settlements, households, regions, etc.) are formally expressed by means of the geometric features of points, lines or areal units (polygons) in a plane, or, less frequently, on a surface. This spatial referencing of observations is also the salient feature of a Geographic Information System (GIS), which makes it a natural tool to aid in the analysis of spatial data. I return to this issue in more detail below.

The crucial role of location for spatial data, both in an absolute sense (coordinates) and in a relative sense (spatial arrangement, distance) has major implications for the way in which they should be treated in statistical analysis, as discussed in detail in Anselin (1990a). Indeed, location gives rise to two classes of socalled spatial effects: spatial dependence and spatial heterogeneity. The first, often also referred to as spatial autocorrelation or spatial association, follows directly from Tobler's (1979) First Law of Geography, according to which "everything is related to everything else, but near things are more related than distant things." As a consequence, similar values for a variable will tend to occur in nearby locations, leading to spatial clusters. For example, a high crime neighborhood in an inner city will often be surrounded by other high crime areas, or a low income county in a remote region may be neighboring other low income counties. This spatial clustering implies that many samples of geographical data will no longer satisfy the usual statistical assumption of independence of observations.

A major consequence of the dependence in a spatial sample is that statistical inference will not be as efficient as for an independent sample of the same size. In other words, the dependence leads to a loss of information.roughly speaking, and everything else being the same, this will be reflected in larger, variances for estimates, lower significance levels in tests of hypotheses and a poorer fit for models estimated with data from dependent samples, compared to independent samples of the same size. I will refer to this aspect of spatial dependence in the rest of the paper as a nuisance. The loss in efficiency may be remedied by increasing the sample size or by designing a sampling scheme that spaces observations such that their interaction is negligible. Alternatively, it may be taken into account by means of specialized statistical methods. In this paper, I will focus on the latter. When spatial dependence is considered to be a nuisance, one only wants to make sure that the interpretation of the results of a statistical analysis are valid. One is thus not really interested in the source of the spatial association, i.e., in the form of the spatial interaction, the characteristics of the spatial structure, or the shape of the spatial and/or social processes that led to the dependence. When the latter is the main concern, I will use the term substantive spatial dependence instead.

The second type of spatial effect, spatial heterogeneity, pertains to the spatial or regional differentiation which follows from the intrinsic uniqueness of each location. This is a special case of the general problem of structural instability. As is well known, in order to draw conclusions with a degree of general validity from the study of a spatial sample, it is necessary that this sample represents some type of equilibrium. In the analysis of cross-sectional data in the social sciences this assumption is typically made. However, this assumption is considered with respect to the time dimension only, and systematic instability or structural variation that may be exhibited across different locations in space is mostly ignored. Such spatial heterogeneity may be evidenced in various aspects of the statistical analysis: it may occur in the form of different distributions holding for spatial, subsets of the data, or more simply, in the form of different means, variances or other parameter values between the subsets. I will refer to discrete changes over the landscape, such as a difference in mean or variance between inner city and suburb, or between northern and southern states as spatial regimes, where each regime corresponds to a well-defined subset of locations. Alternatively, I will call a continuous variation with location spatial drift. This would be the case if the parameters of a distribution vary in a smooth fashion with location, for example, when their mean follows a polynomial expression in the x and y coordinates (this is referred to as a trend surface). As is the case for spatial dependence, spatial heterogeneity can also be considered either as a nuisance or as substantive heterogeneity

Spatial Data Analysis

In Anselin and Griffith (1988), it is shown in some detail how the results of data analyses may become invalid if spatial dependence and/or spatial heterogeneity are ignored. Consequently, specialized techniques must be used instead of those that follow the standard assumptions of independence and homogeneity. By now, a large body of such techniques has been developed, which appears in the literature under the rubrics of spatial statistics, geostatistics, or spatial econometrics. The differences between these "fields" are subtle and to some extent semantic. Spatial statistics is typically considered to be the most general of the three, with geostatistics focused on applications in the physical (geological) sciences, and spatial econometrics finding application in economic modeling.

A useful taxonomy for spatial data analysis was recently suggested by Cressie (1991). He distinguishes between three broad classes of spatial data and identifies a set of specialized techniques for each. Crressie's taxonomy consists of lattice data (discrete variation over space, with observations associated with regular or irregular areal units), geostatistical data (observations associated with a continuous variation over space, typically in function of distance), and point patterns (occurrences of events at locations in space). In the remainder of this paper, I will focus exclusively on the first category (lattice data), due to space limitations, but also because I have found it to be the most appropriate perspective for applications in the social sciences that utilize GIS. I chose not to discuss geostatistics, since the requirement of continuous variation with distance in an isotropic space is typically not satisfied by spatial samples in the social sciences. Such samples are mostly limited to data for areal units, which are often defined in a rather arbitrary fashion, making an assumption of continuity tenuous at best. Recent reviews of geostatistical techniques can be found in Davis (1986), Isaaks and Srivastava (1989), Webster and Oliver (1990), and Cressie (1991). In contrast to the geostatistical data viewpoint, point patterns represent a very appropriate perspective for the study of many phenomena in the social sciences, such as the analysis of the spatial arrangement of settlements, of store locations, occurences of crime, infectuous diseases, etc. I elected not to discuss them in this paper because their study does not require much in terms of the functionality of a GIS, once the coordinates of the locations have been determined. A very readable introduction to point pattern analysis is given in Boots and Getis (1988) and Upton and Fingleton (1985). More advanced treatments can be found in Getis and Boots (1978), Ripley (1981) and Diggle (1983), as well as in Cressie (1991).

Unfortunately, the need for specialized spatial data analysis techniques is not commonly appreciated in empirical work, as illustrated by an analysis of the contents of recent journal issues in regional science and urban economics in Anselin and Hudak(1992).Over 200 empirical articles were reviewed, of which slightly more than one fifth employed spatial data, roughly evenly divided between purely cross-sectional and pooled cross-section and time series data. Of those, only one considered spatial dependence in a rigorous fashion. This absence of a strong dissemination of the methodological findings to the practice of empirical research is often attributed to the lack of operational software for spatial data analysis, e.g., as argued in Haining (1989, p. 201). While this may have been the case in the past, several recent efforts have added features for spatial analysis to many existing statistical and econometric software packages, in the form of macros and special subroutines. A small number of dedicated spatial data analysis software packages have become available as well, which should greatly facilitate the use of these techniques by a wider range of social scientists.

GIS and Spatial Data Analysis

A linkage between GIS and spatial data analysis is considered to be an important aspect in the development of GIS into a research tool to explore and analyze spatial relationships. The limited availability of advanced analytical capabilities in commercial
GIS packages is by now a familiar complaint in the research literature, going back to Goodchild (1987), and several calls for a closer integration between spatial analysis and GIS have been formulated (e.g., Openshaw, 1990). In the past few years, this has resulted in considerable research activity in this area, as evidenced by an increasing number of review articles, conceptual outlines, and guides for practical implementation of the Linkage, e.g., in Anselin

and Getis (1992), Bailey (1992), Fischer and Nijkamp (1992), Goodchild et al. (1992), and Anselin, Dodson and Hudak (1992).

Simply put, the power of a GIS as an aid in spatial data analysis lies in its georelational. Data base structure, i.e., in the combination of value information and locational. Information. The link between these two allows for the fast computation of various characteristics of the spatial arrangement of the data, such as the contiguity structure between observations, which are essential inputs into spatial data analysis. The GIS also provides a flexible means to "create new data," i.e., to transform data between different spatial scales of observation, and to carry out aggregation, partitioning, interpolation, overlay and buffering operations. Of course, such "data" is nothing but the result of computations, themselves based on particular algorithms that often use parameter estimates and model calibrations obtained by statistical means. The powerful display capabilities contained in a GIS also provide excellent tools for the visualization of the results of statistical analyses.

A Short Guide to the Literature

The treatment of spatial data analysis from the lattice data perspective focuses on two main issues: testing for the presence of spatial association, and the estimation of regression models that incorporate spatial effects. Most of the introductory level writings in the field only deal with the former. Examples are selected materials in textbooks on "statistics for geographers," such as in Ebdon (1985) and Griffith and Amrhein (1991), and the small pedagogic volumes devoted to the topic of "spatial autocorrelation" by Griffith (1987) and Odland (1988). A more technical treatment of these issues can be found in the classic works of Cliff and Ord (1973, 1981) and in Upton and Fingleton (1985). In addition to dealing with spatial autocorrelation, these texts also cover several aspects of spatial regression modeling.

A more specific focus on spatial effects in regression analysis can be found in Haining (1990) at the intermediate level, and in Anselin (1988a), Griffith (1988a), and also Cressie (1991) at the more advanced level. An extensive discussion of operational implementation issues, including extensive listings of software code, is given in Anselin and Hudak (1992), and Anselin and Griffith (1993).

A good overview of current research issues in spatial statistics can be found in a publication by the Panel on Spatial Statistics and Image Processing of the National Research Council (NRC, 1991). Other recent sources that include both methodological discussions and empirical applications relevant for spatial data analysis in the social sciences are the volume edited by Griffith (1990), and a special issue of the journal Regional Science and Urban Economics that is devoted to "Space and Applied Econometrics" (Anselin, 1992a).

Empirical Illustration

In order to present the technical materials in this paper in more concrete terms, I will illustrate several of the methods discussed in the following sections with a simple empirical example. I chose to present a partial replication of a study by Ormrod (1990) on the adoption of air conditioners and food freezers in the U.S. in the 1950s, which uses data for a cross-section of the 48 contiguous states. Only the analysis of food freezers will be replicated. I selected this study for two main reasons. Firstly, it illustrates the type of empirical analysis where the focus of interest is on spatial context and spatial interaction, which is typical of many spatial investigations in the social sciences. Secondly, it demonstrates how the careful inclusion of the proper spatial variables into a model may provide important additional insights.

1.1 What title means?

Spatial analysis can perhaps be considered to have arisen with the early attempts at cartography and surveying but many fields have contributed to its rise in modern form. Biology contributed through botanical studies of global plant distributions and local plant locations, ethological studies of animal movement, landscape ecological studies of vegetation blocks, ecological studies of spatial population dynamics, and the study of biogeography. Epidemiology contributed with early work on disease mapping, notably John Snow's work mapping an outbreak of cholera, with research on mapping the spread of disease and with locational studies for health care delivery.

Statistics has contributed greatly through work in spatial statistics. Economics has contributed notably through spatial econometrics. Geographic information system is currently a major contributor due to the importance of geographic software in the modern analytic toolbox. Remote sensing has contributed extensively in morphometric and clustering analysis.

Computer science has contributed extensively through the study of algorithms, notably in computational geometry. Mathematics continues to provide the fundamental tools for analysis and to reveal the complexity of the spatial realm, for example, with recent work on fractals and scale invariance. Scientific modelling provides a useful framework for new approaches.

1.2 Short Description

Spatial analysis or spatial statistics includes any of the formal techniques which study entities using their topological, geometric, or geographic properties. The phrase properly refers to a variety of techniques, many still in their early development, using different analytic approaches and applied in fields as diverse as astronomy, with its studies of the placement of galaxies in the cosmos, to chip fabrication engineering, with its use of 'place and route' algorithms to build complex wiring structures. The phrase is often used in a more restricted sense to describe techniques applied to structures at the human scale, most notably in the analysis of geographic data. The phrase is even sometimes used to refer to a specific technique in a single area of research, for example, to describe geostatistics.

1.3 Advantages / Merits

Spatial databases provide much more efficient storage, retrieval, and analysis of spatial data

Able to treat your spatial data like anything else in the DB
- transactions
- Backups
- less data redundancy
- fundamental organization and operations handled by the DB
- multi-user support
- security/access control
- locking

Use simple SQL expressions to determine spatial relationships
- distance
- adjacency
- containment

Use simple SQL expressions to perform spatial operations
- area
- length
- intersection
- union
- buffer

1.4 Disadvantages / Demerits

Spatial analysis confronts many fundamental issues in the definition of its objects of study, in the construction of the analytic operations to be used, in the use of computers for analysis, in the limitations and particularities of the analyses which are known, and in the presentation of analytic results. Many of these issues are active subjects of modern research.

Common errors often arise in spatial analysis, some due to the mathematics of space, some due to the particular ways data are presented spatially, some due to the tools which are available. Census data, because it protects individual privacy by aggregating data into local units, raises a number of statistical issues. The fractal nature of coastline makes precise measurements of its length difficult if not impossible. A computer software fitting straight lines to the curve of a coastline, can easily calculate the lengths of the lines which it defines. However these straight lines may have no inherent meaning in the real world, as was shown for the coastline of Britain. These problems represent one of the greatest dangers in spatial analysis because of the inherent power of maps as media of presentation. When results are presented as maps, the presentation combines the spatial data which is generally very accurate with analytic results which may be grossly inaccurate. Some of these issues are discussed at length in the book How to Lie with Map.

Spatial characterization

The definition of the spatial presence of an entity constrains the possible analysis which can be applied to that entity and influences the final conclusions that can be reached. While this property is fundamentally true of all analysis, it is particularly important in spatial analysis because the tools to define and study entities favor specific characterizations of the entities being studied. Statistical techniques favor the spatial definition of objects as points because there are very few statistical techniques which operate directly on line, area, or volume elements. Computer tools favor the spatial definition of objects as homogeneous and separate elements because of the limited number of database elements and computational structures available, and the ease with which these primitive structures can be created.

8

Spatial dependency or auto-correlation

Spatial dependency is the co-variation of properties within geographic space: characteristics at proximal locations appear to be correlated, either positively or negatively. Spatial dependency leads to the spatial autocorrelation problem in statistics since, like temporal autocorrelation, this violates standard statistical techniques that assume independence among observations. For example, regression analyses that do not compensate for spatial dependency can have unstable parameter estimates and yield unreliable significance tests. Spatial regression models (see below) capture these relationships and do not suffer from these weaknesses. It is also appropriate to view spatial dependency as a source of information rather than something to be corrected.

Locational effects also manifest as spatial heterogeneity, or the apparent variation in a process with respect to location in geographic space. Unless a space is uniform and boundless, every location will have some degree of uniqueness relative to the other locations. This affects the spatial dependency relations and therefore the spatial process. Spatial heterogeneity means that overall parameters estimated for the entire system may not adequately describe the process at any given location.

Scaling

Spatial measurement scale is a persistent issue in spatial analysis; more detail is available at the modifiable areal unit problem (MAUP) topic entry. Landscape ecologists developed a series of scale invariant metrics for aspects of ecology that are fractal in nature.[citation needed] In more general terms, no scale independent method of analysis is widely agreed upon for spatial statistics.

Sampling

Spatial sampling involves determining a limited number of locations in geographic space for faithfully measuring phenomena that are subject to dependency and heterogeneity.[citation needed]Dependency suggests that since one location can predict the value of another location, we do not need observations in both places. But heterogeneity suggests that this relation can change across space, and therefore we cannot trust an observed degree of dependency beyond a region that may be small. Basic spatial sampling schemes include random, clustered and systematic. These basic schemes can be applied at multiple levels in a designated spatial hierarchy (e.g., urban area, city, neighborhood). It is also possible to exploit ancillary data, for example, using property values as a guide in a spatial sampling scheme to measure educational attainment and income. Spatial models such as autocorrelation statistics, regression and interpolation (see below) can also dictate sample design.

Common errors in spatial analysis

The fundamental issues in spatial analysis lead to numerous problems in analysis including bias, distortion and outright errors in the conclusions reached. These issues are often interlinked but various attempts have been made to separate out particular issues from each other.

Length

In a paper by Benoit Mandelbrot on the coastline of Britain it was shown that it is inherently nonsensical to discuss certain spatial concepts despite an inherent presumption of the validity of the concept. Lengths in ecology depend directly on the scale at which they are measured and experienced. So while surveyors commonly measure the length of a river, this length only has meaning in the context of the relevance of the measuring technique to the question under study.

| Britain measured | Britain measured | Britain measured |
| using a long yardstick | using medium yardstick | using short yardstick |

Locational fallacy

The locational fallacy refers to error due to the particular spatial characterization chosen for the elements of study, in particular choice of placement for the spatial presence of the element.
Spatial characterizations may be simplistic or even wrong. Studies of humans often reduce the spatial existence of humans to a single point, for instance their home address. This can easily lead to poor analysis, for example, when considering disease transmission which can happen at work or at school and therefore far from the home.
The spatial characterization may implicitly limit the subject of study. For example, the spatial analysis of crime data has recently become popular but these studies can only describe the particular kinds of crime which can be described spatially. This leads to many maps of assault but not to any maps of embezzlement with political consequences in the conceptualization of crime and the design of policies to address the issue.

Atomic fallacy

This describes errors due to treating elements as separate 'atoms' outside of their spatial context

Ecological fallacy

The ecological fallacy describes errors due to performing analyses on aggregate data when trying to reach conclusions on the individual units.[citation needed] Errors occur in part from spatial aggregation. For example a pixel represents the average surface temperatures within an area. Ecological fallacy would be to assume that all points within the area have the same temperature. This topic is closely related to the modifiable areal unit problem.

1.5 Solutions to the fundamental issues

Geographic space

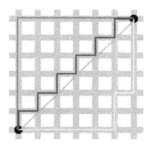

Manhattan distance versus Euclidean distance: The red, blue, and yellow lines have the same length (12) in both Euclidean and taxicab geometry. In Euclidean geometry, the green line has length $6 \times \sqrt{2} \approx 8.48$, and is the unique shortest path. In taxicab geometry, the green line's length is still 12, making it no shorter than any other path shown.

A mathematical space exists whenever we have a set of observations and quantitative measures of their attributes. For example, we can represent individuals' income or years of education within a coordinate system where the location of each individual can be specified with respect to both dimensions. The distances between individuals within this space is a quantitative measure of their differences with respect to income and education. However, in spatial analysis we are concerned with specific types of mathematical spaces, namely, geographic space. In geographic space, the observations correspond to locations in a spatial measurement framework that captures their proximity in the real world. The locations in a spatial measurement framework often represent locations on the surface of the Earth, but this is not strictly necessary. A spatial measurement framework can also capture proximity with respect to, say, interstellar space or within a biological entity such as a liver. The fundamental tenet is Tobler's First Law of Geography: if the interrelation between entities increases with proximity in the real world, then representation in geographic space and assessment using spatial analysis techniques are appropriate.

The Euclidean distance between locations often represents their proximity, although this is only one possibility. There are an infinite number of distances in addition to Euclidean that can support quantitative analysis. For example, "Manhattan" (or "Taxicab") distances where movement is restricted to paths parallel to the axes can be more meaningful than Euclidean distances in urban settings. In addition to distances, other geographic relationships such as connectivity (e.g., the existence or degree of shared borders) and direction can also influence the relationships among entities. It is also possible to compute minimal cost paths across a cost surface; for example, this can represent proximity among locations when travel must occur across rugged terrain.

1.6 Types of spatial analysis

Spatial data comes in many varieties and it is not easy to arrive at a system of classification that is simultaneously exclusive, exhaustive, imaginative, and satisfying. -- G. Upton & B. Fingelton.

Spatial autocorrelation

Spatial autocorrelation statistics measure and analyze the degree of dependency among observations in a geographic space. Classic spatial autocorrelation statistics include Moran's I and Geary's Cand Getis'G. These require measuring a spatial weights matrix that reflects the intensity of the geographic relationship between observations in a neighborhood, e.g., the distances between neighbors, the lengths of shared border, or whether they fall into a specified directional class such as "west". Classic spatial autocorrelation statistics compare the spatial weights to the covariance relationship at pairs of locations. Spatial autocorrelation that is more positive than expected from random indicate the clustering of similar values across geographic space, while significant negative spatial autocorrelation indicates that neighboring values are more dissimilar than expected by chance, suggesting a spatial pattern similar to a chess board.

Spatial autocorrelation statistics such as Moran's I and Geary's C are global in the sense that they estimate the overall degree of spatial autocorrelation for a dataset. The possibility of spatial heterogeneity suggests that the estimated degree of autocorrelation may vary significantly across geographic space. Local spatial autocorrelation statistics provide estimates disaggregated to the level of the spatial analysis units, allowing assessment of the dependency relationships across space. G statistics compare neighborhoods to a global average and identify local regions of strong autocorrelation. Local versions of the I and C statistics are also available.

Spatial interpolation

Spatial interpolation methods estimate the variables at unobserved locations in geographic space based on the values at observed locations. Basic methods include inverse distance weighting: this attenuates the variable with decreasing proximity from the observed location. Kriging is a more sophisticated method that interpolates across space according to a spatial lag relationship that has both systematic and random components. This can accommodate a wide range of spatial relationships for the hidden values between observed locations. Kriging provides optimal estimates given the hypothesized lag relationship, and error estimates can be mapped to determine if spatial patterns exist.

Spatial regression

Spatial regression methods capture spatial dependency in regression analysis, avoiding statistical problems such as unstable parameters and unreliable significance tests, as well as providing information on spatial relationships among the variables involved. Depending on the specific technique, spatial dependency can enter the regression model as relationships between the independent variables and the dependent, between the dependent variables and a spatial lag of itself, or in the error terms. Geographically weighted regression (GWR) is a local version of spatial regression that generates parameters disaggregated by the spatial units of analysis.[citation needed] This allows assessment of the spatial heterogeneity in the estimated relationships between the independent and dependent variables. The use of Markov Chain Monte Carlo (MCMC) methods can allow the estimation of complex functions, such as Poisson-Gamma-CAR, Poisson-lognormal-SAR, or Overdispersed logit models.

Spatial interaction

Spatial interaction or "gravity models" estimate the flow of people, material or information between locations in geographic space. Factors can include origin propulsive variables such as the number of commuters in residential areas, destination attractiveness variables such as the amount of office space in employment areas, and proximity relationships between the locations measured in terms such as driving distance or travel time. In addition, the topological, or connective, relationships between areas must be identified, particularly considering the often conflicting relationship between distance and topology; for example, two spatially close neighborhoods may not display any significant interaction if they are separated by a highway. After specifying the functional forms of these relationships, the analyst can estimate model parameters using observed flow data and standard estimation techniques such as ordinary least squares or maximum likelihood. Competing destinations versions of spatial interaction models include the proximity among the destinations (or origins) in addition to the origin-destination proximity; this captures the effects of destination (origin) clustering on flows. Computational methods such as artificial neural networks can also estimate spatial interaction relationships among locations and can handle noisy and qualitative data.

Simulation and modeling

Spatial interaction models are aggregate and top-down: they specify an overall governing relationship for flow between locations. This characteristic is also shared by urban models such as those based on mathematical programming, flows among economic sectors, or bid-rent theory. An alternative modeling perspective is to represent the system at the highest possible level of disaggregation and study the bottom-up emergence of complex patterns and relationships from behavior and interactions at the individual level.

Complex adaptive systems theory as applied to spatial analysis suggests that simple interactions among proximal entities can lead to intricate, persistent and functional spatial entities at aggregate levels. Two fundamentally spatial simulation methods are cellular automata and agent-based modeling. Cellular automata modeling imposes a fixed spatial framework such as grid cells and specifies rules that dictate the state of a cell based on the states of its neighboring cells. As time progresses, spatial patterns emerge as cells change states based on their neighbors; this alters the conditions for future time periods. For example, cells can represent locations in an urban area and their states can be different types of land use. Patterns that can emerge from the simple interactions of local land uses include office districts and urban sprawl. Agent-based modeling uses software entities (agents) that have purposeful behavior (goals) and can react, interact and modify their environment while seeking their objectives. Unlike the cells in cellular automata, agents can be mobile with respect to space. For example, one could model traffic flow and dynamics using agents representing individual vehicles that try to minimize travel time between specified origins and destinations. While pursuing minimal travel times, the agents must avoid collisions with other vehicles also seeking to minimize their travel times. Cellular automata and agent-based modeling are complementary modeling strategies. They can be integrated into a common geographic automata system where some agents are fixed while others are mobile.

Multiple-Point Geostatistics (MPS)

Spatial analysis of a conceptual geological model is the main purpose of any MPS algorithm. The method analyzes the spatial statistics of the geological model, called the training image, and generates realizations of the phenomena that honor those input multiple-point statistics.
One of the recent technique to accomplish this task is the pattern-based method of Honarkhah.[4] In this method, a distance-based approach is employed to analyze the patterns in the training image. This allows the reproduction of the multiple-point statistics, and the complex geometrical features of the given image. The final generated realizations of this, so called random field, can be used to quantify spatial uncertainty.

1.7 Geographic information science and spatial analysis

Geographic information systems (GIS) and the underlying geographic information science that advances these technologies have a strong influence on spatial analysis. The increasing ability to capture and handle geographic data means that spatial analysis is occurring within increasingly data-rich environments. Geographic data capture systems include remotely sensed imagery, environmental monitoring systems such as intelligent transportation systems, and location-aware technologies such as mobile devices that can report location in near-real time. GIS provide platforms for managing these data, computing spatial relationships such as distance, connectivity and directional relationships between spatial units, and visualizing both the raw data and spatial analytic results within a cartographic context.

Content

- Spatial location: Transfer positioning information of space objects with the help of space coordinate system. Projection transformation theory is the foundation of spatial object representation.
- Spatial distribution: the similar spatial object groups positioning information, including distribution, trends, contrast etc..
- Spatial form: the geometric shape of the spatial objects
- Spatial space: the space objects' approaching degree
- Spatial relationship: relationship between spatial objects,including topological, orientation, similarity, etc..

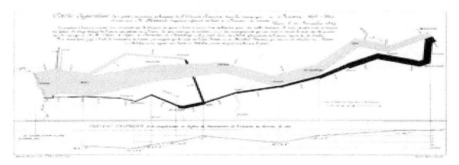

This flow map of Napoleon's ill-fated march on Moscow is an early and celebrated example of geovisualization. It shows the army's direction as it traveled, the places the troops passed through, the size of the army as troops died from hunger and wounds, and the freezing temperatures they experienced.

Geovisualization (GVis) combines scientific visualization with digital cartography to support the exploration and analysis of geographic data and information, including the results of spatial analysis or simulation. GVis leverages the human orientation towards visual information processing in the exploration, analysis and communication of geographic data and information. In contrast with traditional cartography, GVis is typically three or four-dimensional (the latter including time) and user-interactive.

Geographic knowledge discovery (GKD) is the human-centered process of applying efficient computational tools for exploring massivespatial databases. GKD includes geographic data mining, but also encompasses related activities such as data selection, data cleaning and pre-processing, and interpretation of results. GVis can also serve a central role in the GKD process. GKD is based on the premise that massive databases contain interesting (valid, novel, useful and understandable) patterns that standard analytical techniques cannot find. GKD can serve as a hypothesis-generating process for spatial analysis, producing tentative patterns and relationships that should be confirmed using spatial analytical techniques.

Spatial Decision Support Systems (sDSS) take existing spatial data and use a variety of mathematical models to make projections into the future. This allows urban and regional planners to test intervention decisions prior to implementation.

2. Spatial Database System

A spatial database is a database that is optimized to store and query data that is related to objects in space, including points, lines and polygons. While typical databases can understand various numeric and character types of data, additional functionality needs to be added for databases to process spatial data types. These are typically called geometry or feature. The Open Geospatial Consortium created the Simple Features specification and sets standards for adding spatial functionality to database systems.

In various fields there is a need to manage geometric, geographic, or spatial data, which means data related to space. The space of interest can be, for example, the two-dimensional abstraction of (parts of) the surface of the earth – that is, geographic space, the most prominent example –, a man-made space like the layout of a VLSI design, a volume containing a model of the human brain, or another 3d-space representing the arrangement of chains of protein molecules. At least since the advent of relational database systems there have been attempts to manage such data in database systems. Characteristic for the technology emerging to address these needs is the capability to deal with large collections of relatively simple geometric objects, for example, a set of 100 000 polygons. This is somewhat different from areas like CAD databases (solid modeling etc.) where geometric entities are composed hierarchically into complex structures, although the issues are certainly related.

Several terms have been used for database systems offering such support like pictorial, image, geometric, geographic, or spatial database system. The terms "pictorial" and "image" database system arise from the fact that the data to be managed are often initially captured in the form of digital raster images (e.g. remote sensing by satellites, or computer tomography in medical applications). The term "spatial database system" has become popular during the last few years, to some extent through the series of conferences "Symposium on Large Spatial Databases (SSD)" held bi-annually since 1989 [Buch89, GünS91, AbO93], and is associated with a view of a database as containing sets of objects in space rather than images or pictures of a space. Indeed, the requirements and techniques for dealing with objects in space that have identity and well-defined extents, locations, and relationships are rather different from those for dealing with raster images. It has therefore been suggested to clearly distinguish two classes of systems called spatial database systems and image database systems, respectively [GünB90, Fra91]. Image database systems may include analysis techniques to extract objects in space from images, and offer some spatial database functionality, but are also prepared to store, manipulate and retrieve raster images as discrete entities. In this survey we only discuss spatial database systems in the restricted sense. Several papers in this special issue address image database problems and so complement the survey.

What is a spatial database system? We are not aware of a generally accepted definition. The following reflects the author's personal view:

(1) A spatial database system is a database system.
(2) It offers spatial data types (SDTs) in its data model and query language.
(3) It supports spatial data types in its implementation, providing at least spatial indexing and Efficient algorithms for spatial join.

Let us briefly justify these requirements. (1) sounds trivial, but emphasizes the fact that spatial, or geometric, information is in practice always connected with "non-spatial" (e.g. alphanumeric) data. Nobody cares about a special purpose system that is not able to handle all the standard data modeling and querying tasks. Hence a spatial database system is a full-fledged database system with additional capabilities for handling spatial data. (2) Spatial data types, e.g. POINT, LINE, REGION, provide a fundamental abstraction for modeling the structure of geometric entities in space as well as their relationships (l intersects r), properties (area(r) > 1000), and operations (intersection(l, r) – the part of l lying within r). Which types are used may, of course, depend on a class of applications to be supported (e.g. rectangles in VLSI design, surfaces and volumes in 3d). Without spatial data types a system does not offer adequate support in modeling. (3) A system must at least be able to retrieve from a large collection of objects in some space those lying within a particular area without scanning the whole set. Therefore spatial indexing is mandatory. It should also support connecting objects from different classes through some spatial relationship in a better way than by filtering the Cartesian product (at least for those relationships that are important for the application).

The purpose of this survey is to present in a coherent way some of the fundamental problems and their solutions in spatial database systems. The focus is on describing solutions that have been found rather than on listing many open problems. We consider spatial DBMS to provide the underlying database technology for geographic information systems (GIS) and other applications. As such, they can offer only some basic capabilities; it is not claimed that a spatial DBMS is directly usable as an application-oriented GIS.

In the following four sections we consider modeling, querying, tools for implementation (data structures and algorithms), and system architecture for spatial database systems.

17

3. Features of Spatial Databases

Database systems use indexes to quickly look up values and the way that most databases index data is not optimal for spatial queries. Instead, spatial databases use a spatial index to speed up database operations.

In addition to typical SQL queries such as SELECT statements, spatial databases can perform a wide variety of spatial operations. The following query types and many more are supported by the Open Geospatial Consortium:

- Spatial Measurements: Finds the distance between points, polygon area, etc.
- Spatial Functions: Modify existing features to create new ones, for example by providing a buffer around them, intersecting features, etc.
- Spatial Predicates: Allows true/false queries such as 'is there a residence located within a mile of the area we are planning to build the landfill?' (see DE-9IM)
- Constructor Functions: Creates new features with an SQL query specifying the vertices (points of nodes) which can make up lines. If the first and last vertex of a line are identical the feature can also be of the type polygon (a closed line).
- Observer Functions: Queries which return specific information about a feature such as the location of the center of a circle

Not all spatial databases support these query types: many support simplified or modified sets, especially in cases of NoSQL systems like MongoDB and CouchDB.

3.1 Spatial Index

Spatial indexes are used by spatial databases (databases which store information related to objects in space) to optimize spatial queries. Indexes used by non-spatial databases cannot effectively handle features such as how far two points differ and whether points fall within a spatial area of interest. Common spatial index methods include:

- Grid (spatial index)
- Z-order (curve)
- Quadtree
- Octree
- UB-tree
- R-tree: Typically the preferred method for indexing spatial data. Objects (shapes, lines and points) are grouped using the minimum bounding rectangle (MBR). Objects are added to an MBR within the index that will lead to the smallest increase in its size.
- R+ tree
- R* tree
- Hilbert R-tree
- X-tree
- kd-tree

- m-tree - an m-tree index can be used for the efficient resolution of similarity queries on complex objects as compared using an arbitrary metric.

3.2 Spatial database systems

- All OpenGIS Specifications compliant products[2]
- Open source spatial databases and APIs, some of which are OpenGIS compliant[3]
- Boeing's Spatial Query Server spatially enables Sybase ASE.
- Smallworld VMDS, the native GE Smallworld GIS database
- SpatiaLite extends Sqlite with spatial datatypes, functions, and utilities.
- IBM DB2 Spatial Extender can be used to enable any edition of DB2, including the free DB2 Express-C, with support for spatial types
- Oracle Spatial
- Microsoft SQL Server has support for spatial types since version 2008
- PostgreSQL DBMS (database management system) uses the spatial extension PostGIS to implement the standardized datatype geometry and corresponding functions.
- MySQL DBMS implements the datatype geometry plus some spatial functions that haven't been implemented according to the OpenGIS specifications. Functions that test spatial relationships are limited to working with minimum bounding rectangles rather than the actual geometries. MySQL versions earlier than 5.0.16 only supported spatial data in MyISAM tables. As of MySQL 5.0.16, InnoDB, NDB, BDB, and ARCHIVE also support spatial features.
- Neo4j - Graph database that can build 1D and 2D indexes as Btree, Quadtree and Hilbert curve directly in the graph
- AllegroGraph - a Graph database provides a novel mechanism for efficient storage and retrieval of two-dimensional geospatial coordinates for Resource Description Framework data. It includes an extension syntax for SPARQL queries
- MongoDB supports geospatial indexes in 2D

3.3 Spatial Queries

A spatial query is a special type of database query supported by geodatabases and spatial databases. The queries differ from SQL queries in several important ways. Two of the most important are that they allow for the use of geometry data types such as points, lines and polygons and that these queries consider the spatial relationship between these geometries.

Types of queries

The function names for queries differ across geodatabases. The following list contains commonly used functions built into PostGIS, a free geodatabase which is a PostgreSQL extension (the term 'geometry' refers to a point, line, box or other two or three dimensional shape):

- Function prototype: functionName (parameter(s)) : return type
- Distance(geometry, geometry) : number
- Equals(geometry, geometry) : boolean
- Disjoint(geometry, geometry) : boolean
- Intersects(geometry, geometry) : boolean
- Touches(geometry, geometry) : boolean
- Crosses(geometry, geometry) : boolean
- Overlaps(geometry, geometry) : boolean
- Contains(geometry, geometry) : boolean
- Length(geometry) : number
- Area(geometry) : number
- Centroid(geometry) : geometry

3.4 Open Geospatial Consortium

The Open Geospatial Consortium (OGC), an international voluntary consensus standards organization, originated in 1994. In the OGC, more than 400 commercial, governmental, nonprofit and research organizations worldwide collaborate in a consensus process encouraging development and implementation of open standards for geospatial content and services, GIS data processing and data sharing.

History

A predecessor organization, OGF, the Open GRASS Foundation, started in 1992 From 1994 to 2004 the organization also used the name Open GIS Consortium

Standards

Most of the OGC standards depend on a generalized architecture captured in a set of documents collectively called the Abstract Specification, which describes a basic data model for representinggeographic features. Atop the Abstract Specification members have developed and continue to develop a growing number of specifications, or standards to serve specific needs for interoperable location and geospatial technology, including GIS.

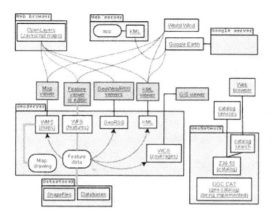

Relationship between clients/servers and some OGC protocols

The OGC standards baseline comprises more than 30 standards, including:

- CSW - Catalog Service for the Web: access to catalog information
- GML - Geography Markup Language: XML-format for geographical information
- GeoXACML - Geospatial eXtensible Access Control Markup Language (as of 2009 in the process of standardization)
- KML - Keyhole Markup Language: XML-based language schema for expressing geographic annotation and visualization on existing (or future) Web-based, two-dimensional maps and three-dimensional Earth browsers
- Observations and Measurements
- OGC Reference Model - a complete set of reference models
- OWS - OGC Web Service Common
- SOS - Sensor Observation Service[4]
- SPS - Sensor Planning Service[5]
- SensorML - Sensor Model Language
- SFS - Simple Features - SQL
- Styled Layer Descriptor (SLD)
- WCS - Web Coverage Service: provides coverage objects from a specified region
- WFS - Web Feature Service: for retrieving or altering feature descriptions
- WMS - Web Map Service: provides map images
- WMTS - Web Map Tile Service: provides map image tiles
- WPS - Web Processing Service: remote processing service

The design of standards were originally built on the HTTP web services paradigm for message-based interactions in web-based systems. However, in the last year[vague] the members have started working on defining a common approach for SOAP protocol and WSDL bindings.

Considerable progress has been made in defining Representational State Transfer (REST) web services.

Organization structure

The OGC has three operational units:

- the Specification program
- the Interoperability Program
- Outreach and Community Adoption

Collaboration

The OGC has a close relationship with ISO/TC 211 (Geographic Information/Geomatics). Volumes from the ISO 19100 series under development by this committee progressively replace the OGC abstract specification. Further, the OGC standards Web Map Service, GML, Web Feature Service, Observations and Measurements, and Simple Features Access have become ISO standards.

The OGC works with more than 20 international standards-bodies including W3C, OASIS, WfMC, and the IETF.

4. SDBMS

Spatial Database Management System (SDBMS) provides the capabilities of a traditional database management system (DBMS) while allowing special storage and handling of spatial data.

SDBMS:

- Works with an underlying DBMS
- Allows spatial data models and types
- Supports querying language specific to spatial data types
- Provides handling of spatial data and operations

A spatial database system:

- Is a database system
  - A DBMS with additional capabilities for handling spatial data
- Offers spatial data types (SDTs) in its data model and query language
  - Structure in space: e.g., POINT, LINE, REGION
  - Relationships among them: (*l intersects r*)
- Supports SDT in its implementation providing at least
  - spatial indexing (retrieving objects in particular area without scanning the whole space)
  - efficient algorithms for spatial joins (not simply filtering the cartesian product)

4.1 SDBMS Three-layer Structure

SDBMS works with a spatial application at the front end and a DBMS at the back end

SDBMS has three layers:

- Interface to spatial application
- Core spatial functionality
- Interface to DBMS

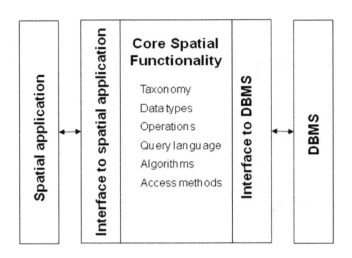

5 Spatial Query Language

Number of specialized adaptations of SQL
- Spatial query language
- Temporal query language (TSQL2)
- Object query language (OQL)
- Object oriented structured query language (O2SQL)

Spatial query language provides tools and structures specifically for working with spatial data
SQL3 provides 2D geospatial types and functions.

5.1 Spatial Query Language Operations

> Three types of queries:

- Basic operations on all data types (e.g. IsEmpty, Envelope, Boundary)

- Topological/set operators (e.g. Disjoint, Touch, Contains)

- Spatial analysis (e.g. Distance, Intersection, SymmDiff)

The following query types and many more are supported by the Open Geospatial Consortium:

- Spatial Measurements: Finds the distance between points, polygon area, etc.
- Spatial Functions: Modify existing features to create new ones, for example by providing a buffer around them, intersecting features, etc.
- Spatial Predicates: Allows true/false queries such as 'is there a residence located within a mile of the area we are planning to build the landfill?'
- Constructor Functions: Creates new features with an SQL query specifying the vertices (points of nodes) which can make up lines. If the first and last vertex of a line are identical the feature can also be of the type polygon (a closed line).
- Observer Functions: Queries which return specific information about a feature such as the location of the center of a circle

Types of Queries – Post GIS

The function names for queries differ across geodatabases. The following list contains commonly used functions built into PostGIS, a free geodatabase which is a PostgreSQL extension (the term 'geometry' refers to a point, line, box or other two or three dimensional shape):

- Distance(geometry, geometry) : number
- Equals(geometry, geometry) : boolean

- Disjoint(geometry, geometry) : boolean
- Intersects(geometry, geometry) : boolean
- Touches(geometry, geometry) : boolean
- Crosses(geometry, geometry) : boolean
- Overlaps(geometry, geometry) : boolean
- Contains(geometry, geometry) : boolean
- Intersects(geometry, geometry) : boolean
- Length(geometry) : number
- Area(geometry) : number
- Centroid(geometry) : geometry

5.2 Spatial Data Entity Creation

Form an entity to hold county names, states, populations, and geographies

```
CREATE TABLE County(
        Name   varchar(30),
        State   varchar(30),
        Pop            Integer,
        Shape  Polygon);
```

Form an entity to hold river names, sources, lengths, and geographies

```
CREATE TABLE River(
        Name   varchar(30),
        Source varchar(30),
        Distance        Integer,
        Shape  LineString);
```

Example Spatial Query

- **Find all the counties that border on Contra Costa county**

```
SELECT      C1.Name
FROM        County C1, County C2
WHERE       Touch(C1.Shape, C2.Shape) = 1 AND C2.Name = 'Contra Costa';
```

- **Find all the counties through which the Merced river runs**

```
SELECT      C.Name, R.Name
FROM        County C, River R
WHERE       Intersect(C.Shape, R.Shape) = 1 AND R.Name = 'Merced';
```

5.3 Features of Spatial Database

- Database systems use indexes to quickly look up values and the way that most databases index data is not optimal for spatial queries. Instead, spatial databases use a spatial index to speed up database operations.
- In addition to typical SQL queries such as SELECT statements, spatial databases can perform a wide variety of spatial operations.

6. Modeling

6.1 What needs to be represented?

The main application driving research in spatial database systems are GIS. Hence we consider some modeling needs in this area which are typical also for other applications. Examples are given for two-dimensional space, but almost everywhere, extension to the three- or more-dimensional case is possible. There are two important alternative views of what needs to be represented:

(i) Objects in space: We are interested in distinct entities arranged in space each of which has its own geometric description.

(ii) Space: We wish to describe space itself, that is, say something about every point in space.
The first view allows one to model, for example, cities, forests, or rivers. The second view is the one of thematic maps describing e.g. land use or the partition of a country into districts. Since raster images say something about every point in space, they are also closely related to the second view. We can reconcile both views to some extent by offering concepts for modeling (i) single objects, and (ii) spatially related collections of objects.

For modeling single objects, the fundamental abstractions are point, line, and region. A point represents (the geometric aspect of) an object for which only its location in space, but not its extent, is relevant. For example, a city may be modeled as a point in a model describing a large geographic area (a large scale map). A line (in this context always to be understood as meaning a curve in space, usually represented by a polyline, a sequence of line segments) is the basic abstraction for facilities for moving through space, or connections in space (roads, rivers, cables for phone, electricity, etc.). A region is the abstraction for something having an extent in 2d-space, e.g. a country, a lake, or a national park. A region may have holes and may also consist of several disjoint pieces. Figure 1 shows the three basic abstractions for single objects.

Figure 1: The three basic abstractions point, line, and region

The two most important instances of spatially related collections of objects are partitions (of the plane) and networks (Figure 2). A partition can be viewed as a set of region objects that are required to be disjoint. The adjacency relationship is of particular interest, that is, there exist often pairs of region objects with a common boundary. Partitions can be used to represent thematic maps. A network can be viewed as a graph embedded into the plane, consisting of a set of point objects, forming its nodes, and a set of line objects describing the geometry of the edges. Networks are ubiquitous in geography, for example, highways, rivers, public transport, or power supply lines.

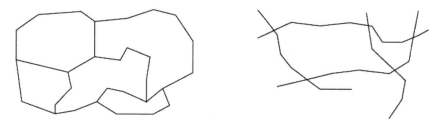

Figure 2: Partitions and networks

Obviously, we have mentioned only the most fundamental abstractions to be supported in a spatial DBMS (for GIS, in this case). For example, other interesting spatially related collections of objects are nested partitions (e.g. a country partitioned into provinces partitioned into districts etc.) or a digital terrain (elevation) model. For a deeper discussion of modeling requirements for GIS. In the sequel we shall consider how the basic abstractions mentioned above can be embedded into a DBMS data model.

6.2 Organizing the Underlying Space: Discrete Geometric Bases

As a basis for geometric modeling very often Euclidean space is used or implicitly assumed. Essentially this means that a point in the plane is given by a pair of real numbers. Unfortunately, in practice, there are no real numbers in computers but only finite and mostly rather limited approximations. This leads to a lot of problems in geometric computation. For example, the intersection point of two lines will be rounded to the nearest grid (that is, representable) point; a subsequent test whether the intersection point is on one of the lines yields false. If the fact that finite representations are used is ignored in modeling, these problems are left to the implementor of a spatial DBMS, which will rather inevitably lead to errors in query processing. Some authors have therefore suggested to introduce a discrete geometric basis for modeling as well as implementation.

The approach of [FraK86, EgFJ89] is based on combinatorial topology. Basic concepts are those of a simplex, and a simplicial complex. For each dimension d, a d-simplex is a minimal object in that dimension, hence a 0-simplex is a point, a 1-simplex is a line segment, a 2-simplex a triangle, a 3simplex a tetrahedron, etc. Any d-simplex is composed of (d+1) simplices of dimension d-1. For example, a triangle, a 2-simplex, is composed of 3 1-simplices (line segments), a line segment as a 1simplex is composed of 2 0-simplices (points). The components used in the composition of a simplex are called its faces (for a triangle its edges and vertices). A simplicial complex is a finite set of simplices such that the intersection of any two simplices in the set is a face. Figure 3 shows a 1complex and a 2-complex.

29

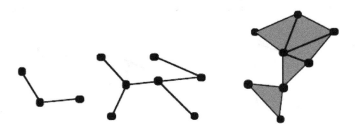

Figure 3: Two simplicial complexes

An alternative proposal of a discrete geometric basis is the concept of a realm [GütS93a]. A realm conceptually represents the complete underlying geometry of one particular application space (in two dimensions). Formally, a realm is a finite set of points and line segments over a discrete grid such that (i) each point or end point of a line segment is a grid point, (ii) each end point of a line segment is also a point of the realm, (iii) no realm point lies within a line segment (which means on it without being an end point), and (iv) no two realm segments intersect except at their end points. Figure 4 illustrates a realm.

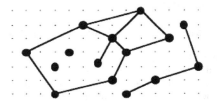

Figure 4: A realm

With both approaches, the idea is now to form the geometries of application objects by composing the primitives of the underlying geometric base. One can easily see how the point, line, or region objects of Section 2.1 can be described in terms of simplices or of the elements of a realm. Furthermore, if spatially related collections of objects such as partitions or networks are represented on top of such a geometric base, then consistency of shared geometries and to some extent relationships between objects are automatically provided by this base layer. Numeric robustness problems can be treated within the geometric base layer so that spatial data types or algebras defined on top enjoy nice closure properties not only in theory but also in an implementation .

6.3 Spatial Data Types

Systems of spatial data types, or spatial algebras, can capture the fundamental abstractions for point, line and region described above together with relationships between them and operations for composition (e.g. forming the intersection of regions). We have stated in Section 1 that they are a mandatory part of the data model for a spatial DBMS, so that indeed, all proposals for models and query languages as well as prototype systems offer them in some form. Spatial types and operations have, for example, been described in,some dedicated work towards a formal definition has been reported . As an example spatial algebra we briefly consider the ROSE algebra.

The ROSE algebra offers three data types called points, lines, and regions, whose values are realm-based, that is, composed from elements of a realm. To describe these values, one needs intermediate notions of an R-block and an R-face. For a given realm R, an R-block is a connected set of line segments of R. An R-face is essentially a polygon with holes that can be defined over realm segments. Then a value of type points is a set of R-points, a value of type lines is a set of disjoint R-blocks, and a value of type regions is a set of edge-disjoint R-faces (edge-disjoint means two faces may have a common vertex, but no common edge).

The type system of the ROSE algebra is based on second-order signature [Güt93] which allows one to describe polymorphic operations by quantification over kinds (which can here just be viewed as type sets). Two such sets are EXT = {lines, regions} and GEO = {points, lines, regions}. There are four classes of operations; for each of them we show a few examples:

(1) Spatial predicates expressing topological relationships:

$$\forall \ geo \ \text{in GEO.} \ \forall \ ext_1, ext_2 \ \text{in EXT.} \ \forall \ area \ \text{in} \ \underline{regions}^{area\text{-}disjoint}.$$

$geo \times \underline{regions}$	$\rightarrow \underline{bool}$	**inside**
$ext_1 \times ext_2$	$\rightarrow \underline{bool}$	**intersects, meets**
$area \times area$	$\rightarrow \underline{bool}$	**adjacent, encloses**

Here the type variable geo ranges over the three types in kind GEO, so that the inside operation can compare a points, a lines, or a regions value with a regions value. The intersects operation can be applied to two values of the same or different types within kind EXT. The notation regions[areadisjoint] is an attempt to capture the structure of partitions in the type system. It describes a kind for all partitions; each particular partition (thematic map) is a type within this kind whose values are the regions within this partition. Hence the type variable area will pick one partition and the operation adjacent be applicable to any two regions of that partition.

(2) Operations returning atomic spatial data type values:

$\forall$ *geo* in GEO.

lines $\times$ *lines*	$\rightarrow$ *points*	**intersection**
regions $\times$ *regions*	$\rightarrow$ *regions*	**intersection**
geo $\times$ *geo*	$\rightarrow$ *geo*	**plus, minus**
regions	$\rightarrow$ *lines*	**contour**

Here plus and minus form the union and difference, respectively, of two values of the same type.

(3) Spatial operators returning numbers:

$\forall$ *geo*$_1$ $\times$ *geo*$_2$ in GEO.

geo$_1$ $\times$ *geo*$_2$	$\rightarrow$ *real*	**dist**
regions	$\rightarrow$ *real*	**perimeter, area**

(4) Spatial operations on set of objects:

$\forall$ *obj* in OBJ.$\forall$ *geo, geo*$_1$, *geo*$_2$ in GEO.

set(*obj*) $\times$ (*obj* $\rightarrow$ *geo*)	$\rightarrow$ *geo*	**sum**
set(*obj*) $\times$ (*obj* $\rightarrow$ *geo*$_1$) $\times$ *geo*$_2$	$\rightarrow$ *set*(*obj*)	**closest**

Here sum is a "spatial aggregate function". It takes a set of objects together with a spatial attribute of the objects of type geo (given as a function mapping each object into its attribute value) and returns the geometric union of all attribute values. For example, one might form the union of a set of provinces to determine the area of a country. The closest operator determines within a set of objects those whose spatial attribute value has minimal distance from some other geometric (query) object.

These examples may suffice to show the kinds of operations that may be available in a spatial algebra. Formal definitions of the semantics of these types and operations can be found. Some important issues related to spatial data types or algebras are the following:

- Extensibility. There is general agreement, that the definition of types and, in particular, operations, is application-dependent. Hence it must be possible to define additional or alternative types and operations later which leads to the requirement of extensibility for the system architecture.

- Completeness. Nevertheless, the question is whether there are any formal criteria to say that a particular collection of operations is complete in some respect. Some limited success in this direction has been obtained in the study of topological relationships.
- One or more types? Is it really necessary to have several different types, to distinguish, for example, points, lines, and regions? Some authors suggest to offer just a single type geometry whose instances can be any of these or even mixed collections of them. This is analogous to the question whether a system should offer different types integer and real, or just a single type number. One advantage of a single type may be that closure under operations is easier to achieve. On the other hand, several types are more expressive and allow a more precise application of operations.
- Set Operations. A spatial algebra should offer not only operations on "atomic" SDT values (a region value is considered to be atomic, even if it has a very large description) but also on spatially related sets of objects, for example, a partition (thematic map, tesselation). Example operations are overlay of two partitions, fusion (merging adjacent areas in a partition if other attributes are equal), or finding in a set of objects the one closest to a query object. This kind of operations requires a much more intricate interfacing with the DBMS data model than in the case of atomic operations.

6.4 Spatial Relationships

Among the operations offered by spatial algebras, spatial relationships are the most important ones. For example, they make it possible to ask for all objects in a given relationship with a query object, e.g. all objects within a window. One can distinguish several classes:

- Topological relationships, such as adjacent, inside, disjoint, are invariant under topological transformations like translation, scaling, and rotation.
- Direction relationships, for example, above, below, or north_of, southwest_of, etc.
- Metric relationships, e.g. "distance < 100".

Among these, topological relationships are most fundamental and have been studied in some depth. A basic question is whether we can somehow enumerate all possible relationships. A method for this was proposed in [Eg89, EgH90]. It was originally formulated for simple regions (connected, no holes), called area in the sequel, and is based on comparing the intersections of their boundaries and interiors (denoted ∂A and $A°$, respectively). For two objects there are 4 intersection sets; each of them may be empty or non-empty which leads to $2^4 = 16$ combinations. These are listed in Table 1. It turns out that 8 of these are not valid and two of them symmetric so that 6 different relationships result, called disjoint, in, touch, equal, cover, and overlap. This approach has been extended in various ways. For example, point and line features have been added [EgH92, HoO92]. Egenhofer has extended the original 4-intersection method to a 9-intersection method by considering also intersections with the complement A-1 [Eg91b]. Clementini et al. [ClFO93] also consider the dimension of the intersection (called the dimension-extended method); in 2d-space the intersection can be empty, 0D (point), 1D (line), or 2D (area). This results in principle in $4^4 = 256$ combinations. Again, many of these are not valid, so that in total 52 relationships among point, line, and area features remain.

$\partial A_1 \cap \partial A_2$	$\partial A_1 \cap A_2^\circ$	$A_1^\circ \cap \partial A_2$	$A_1^\circ \cap A_2^\circ$	relationship name
$\varnothing$	$\varnothing$	$\varnothing$	$\varnothing$	A_1 disjoint A_2
$\varnothing$	$\varnothing$	$\varnothing$	$\neq\varnothing$	
$\varnothing$	$\varnothing$	$\neq\varnothing$	$\varnothing$	
$\varnothing$	$\varnothing$	$\neq\varnothing$	$\neq\varnothing$	A_2 in A_1
$\varnothing$	$\neq\varnothing$	$\varnothing$	$\varnothing$	
$\varnothing$	$\neq\varnothing$	$\varnothing$	$\neq\varnothing$	A_1 in A_2
$\varnothing$	$\neq\varnothing$	$\neq\varnothing$	$\varnothing$	
$\varnothing$	$\neq\varnothing$	$\neq\varnothing$	$\neq\varnothing$	
$\neq\varnothing$	$\varnothing$	$\varnothing$	$\varnothing$	A_1 touch A_2
$\neq\varnothing$	$\varnothing$	$\varnothing$	$\neq\varnothing$	A_1 equal A_2
$\neq\varnothing$	$\varnothing$	$\neq\varnothing$	$\varnothing$	
$\neq\varnothing$	$\varnothing$	$\neq\varnothing$	$\neq\varnothing$	A_1 cover A_2
$\neq\varnothing$	$\neq\varnothing$	$\varnothing$	$\varnothing$	
$\neq\varnothing$	$\neq\varnothing$	$\varnothing$	$\neq\varnothing$	A_2 cover A_1
$\neq\varnothing$	$\neq\varnothing$	$\neq\varnothing$	$\varnothing$	
$\neq\varnothing$	$\neq\varnothing$	$\neq\varnothing$	$\neq\varnothing$	A_1 overlap A_2

Table 1: Enumerating topological relationships by intersections of boundaries and interiors

Since these are far too many to be named and remembered by a user, an alternative is suggested. Five basic relationship names are introduced (touch, in, cross, overlap, and disjoint) whose meaning is formally defined in terms of the dimension extended method, for example:

The touch relationship applies to area/area, line/line, line/area, point/area, and point/line, but not point/point situations. For two features 11 and 12 it is defined by:

$$\langle \lambda_1 \text{ touch } \lambda_2 \rangle : \Leftrightarrow (\lambda_1^\circ \cap \lambda_2^\circ = \varnothing) \wedge (\lambda_1 \cap \lambda_2 \neq \varnothing)$$

In addition to the five relationships, three operators are offered to get the boundaries of features: operator b applied to area A yields the boundary line ∂A; operators f and t return the end points of a line. It is proved in [ClFO93] that the five relationships are mutually exclusive (no two different relationships can hold between any two features) and that all situations described by the dimension-extended method can be distinguished using the relationships and the three boundary operators. – Other work on spatial relationships includes [Fr91, Fra92, CuKR93]. The paper by Papadias and Sellis in this special issue investigates the subject in more depth; further references can be found there.

6.5 Integrating Geometry into the DBMS Data Model

The central idea for integrating geometric modeling into a DBMS data model is to represent "spatial objects" (in the sense of application objects such as river, country, city, etc.) by objects (in the sense of the DBMS data model) with at least one attribute of a spatial data type. Hence the DBMS data model must be extended by SDTs at the level of atomic data types (such as integer, string, etc.), or better be generally open for user-defined types ("abstract data type support" [StRG83]). So far, most often the relational model has been used as a basis (e.g. [ChF80, Güt88, RoFS88, OoSM89, Eg94]) but the approach can be used as well with any other, e.g. object-oriented, data model. In the relational case an object is represented by a tuple, so we can define example relations (of course, real GIS deal with less trivial application objects):

Relation states (sname: STRING; area: REGION; spop: INTEGER)

Relation cities (cname: STRING; center: POINT; ext: REGION; cpop: INTEGER)

Relation rivers (rname: STRING; route: LINE)

In [LiN87], SDTs have been integrated into an extended ER model, in [ScV89] into a complex object model. More difficult is the question how we can handle partitions and networks (Section 2.1). For partitions, it is of course possible to view them just as sets of objects with region attributes. But then the information is lost that regions should be disjoint and that adjacency relationships are of particular importance within this class (which might be used, for example, for establishing "adjacency join indices"). The importance of modeling and manipulating partitions was emphasized e.g. in [MaC80, Fra88, Güt88, ScV89, To90]. In [Güt88] it was suggested to introduce a special AREA data type; creating a relation with an attribute of type AREA would imply that all regions occurring as values of this relation had to be disjoint. But this is not clean since it abuses the concept of a data type to describe what should really be an integrity constraint on a relation.

The modeling of spatially embedded networks has not yet received much attention in the research literature, although quite a bit of work has been done for graphs in databases in general (e.g. [Ag87, Rose86, CrMW87, GyPV90]). Usually the assumption is that graphs are represented by the given facilities of a data model. A disadvantage is then that the graph structure is not visible to the user and can not be supported very well in system implementation. In [Güt94] the GraphDB model is proposed, which emphasizes an explicit modeling of graphs together with a clean integration into a "standard" object-oriented model. GraphDB offers object classes with inheritance, like other OO models, but additionally distinguishes three kinds of object classes called simple classes, link classes and path classes, whose elements correspond to nodes, edges, and explicitly stored paths of a graph. For example, in GraphDB we can model a highway network whose nodes are highway junctions and exits with an associated POINT attribute, whose edges are highway sections with an associated LINE attribute, and where highways are explicitly stored paths, as follows:

```
class vertex = pos: POINT;
vertex class junction = name: STRING;
vertex class exit = nr: INTEGER;
link class section = route: LINE, no_lanes: INTEGER, top_speed: INTEGER
from vertex to vertex;
path class highway = name: STRING as section+;
```

Here the junction and exit subclasses inherit the pos attibute from the vertex class. A highway is a path over a non-empty sequence of section edges. For further details see [Güt94]. Another spatial data model with explicit graphs is described in [ErG91].

7 Querying

From one point of view, the problem of querying is to connect the operations of a spatial algebra (including predicates to express spatial relationships) to the facilities of a DBMS query language. But there are also other aspects that have mainly to do with the fact that spatial data require a graphical presentation of results as well as graphical input of queries or at least SDT values used in queries. In the following three subsections, we consider the fundamental operations needed at the level of manipulating sets of database objects, graphical input and output, and techniques and requirements for extending query languages.

7.1 Fundamental Operations (Algebra)

We now consider from an algebraic point of view operations for manipulating sets of database objects with spatial attributes. They can be classified as spatial selection, spatial join, spatial function application, and other set operations.

Spatial Selection. Strictly speaking, there is no such thing as a spatial selection. A selection is an operation that returns from a set of objects those fulfilling a predicate. However, the term is used in the literature to describe a selection based on a spatial predicate (e.g. [ArS91a]). Some examples:

"Find all cities in Bavaria" (assuming Bavaria exists as a REGION value and inside is available in the spatial algebra)

cities select[center inside Bavaria]

"Find all rivers intersecting a query window."

rivers select[route intersects Window]

"Find all big cities no more than 100 kms from Hagen" (Hagen being a POINT value).

cities select[dist(center, Hagen) < 100 and pop > 500000]

The last example illustrates that selection conditions can also be based on metric relationships and can occur in conjunction with other predicates. Query optimization should be able to compare access plans using spatial indices with plans using a standard index.

Spatial Join. Similarly to a spatial selection, a spatial join is a join which compares any two objects through a predicate on their spatial attribute values. Some examples:

"Combine cities with their states."

cities states join[center inside area]

"For each river, find all cities within less than 50 kms."

cities rivers join[dist(center, route) < 50]

As mentioned in Section 1, spatial selection and spatial join are so important that it is mandatory to support them by spatial indexing and by special join algorithms, at least for the most important spatial predicates.

Spatial Function Application. How can operations of a spatial algebra computing new SDT values (class 2 in Section 2.3) be used in a query? In a set-oriented query a new SDT value is computed for each object in a set. Various object algebra operators allow such an embedding of a function application, for example, the filter operator of FAD [Banc87], a replace operator in [AbB88], or the l or extend operator of [GütZC89]. The extend operator takes an expression to be evaluated for each object and a (new) attribute name; it appends the resulting value as a new attribute to the object. For example:

"For each river going through Bavaria, return the name, the part of its geometry lying inside Bavaria, and the length of that part."

rivers select[route intersects Bavaria]

extend[intersection(route, Bavaria) {part}]

extend[length(part) {plength}] project[rname, part, plength]

Other Set Operations. Such operations manipulate whole sets of spatial objects in a special way; they lie at the interface between a spatial algebra and the DBMS object algebra. Of particular importance are operations for the manipulation of partitions (thematic maps); a collection of such operations is described in [ScV89], closely related is the map algebra by Tomlin [To90]. Some suggested operations are the following:

- Overlay. Computes the elementary regions resulting from overlaying two partitions. It can be viewed as a special kind of spatial join [Fra88, Güt88, ScV89].
- Fusion. This is a special kind of grouping. Objects are grouped by some arbitrary attribute values. For each resulting group of objects, the union of all values of a spatial attribute is formed. For example, given a set of region objects with a "land-use" attribute, one can group by land-use to obtain one object for land-use "wheat" with the associated union region, etc. [ScV89, GaNT91].
- Voronoi. Computes from a set S of point objects a corresponding set of region objects (the Voronoi diagram). For each point p, the region consists of the points of the plane closer to p than to any other point in S [Güt88].

7.2 Graphical Input and Output

Traditional database systems deal with alphanumeric data types whose values can easily be entered through a keybord and represented textually within a query result (e.g. a table). For a spatial database system, at least when it is to be used interactively, graphical presentation of SDT values in query results is essential, and entering SDT values to be used as "constants" in queries via a graphical input device is also important. Besides graphical representation of SDT values, another distinctive characteristic of querying a spatial database is that the goal of querying is in general to obtain a "tailored" picture of the space represented in the database, which means that the information to be retrieved is often not the result of a single query but rather a combination of several queries. For example, for GIS applications, the user wants to see a map built by overlaying graphically the results of several queries.

Requirements for spatial querying have been analyzed in [Fra82, EgF88, Eg94]. In [Eg94] the following list is given:

- Spatial data types.
- Graphical display of query results.
- Graphical combination (overlay) of several query results. It should be possible to start a new picture, to add a layer, or to remove a layer from the current display. (Some systems also allow to change the order of layers [Vo91, ViO92]).
- Display of context. To interpret the result of a query, e.g. a point describing the location of a city, it is necessary to show some background, such as the boundary of a state containing it [Fra82]. A raster image of the area can also nicely serve as a background.
-
  A facility for checking the content of a display. When a picture (a map) has been composed by several queries, one should be able to check which queries have built it.
- Extended dialog. It should be possible to use pointing devices to select objects within a picture or subareas (zooming in), e.g. by dragging a rectangle over the picture.
- Varying graphical representations. It should be possible to assign different graphical representations (colors, patterns, intensity, symbols) to different object classes in a picture, or even to distinguish objects within one class (e.g. use different symbols to distinguish cities by population).
- A legend should explain the assignment of graphical representations to object classes.
- Label placement. It should be possible to select object attributes to be used as labels within a graphical representation. Sophisticated ("nice") label placement for a map is a difficult problem, however [FrA87].
- Scale selection. At least for GIS applications, selecting subareas should be based on commonly used map scales. The scale determines not only the size of the graphical representation, but possibly also what kind of symbol is used or whether an object is shown at all (cartographic generalization).
- Subarea for queries. It should be possible to restrict attention to a particular area of the space for several following queries.

These requirements can in general be fulfilled by offering textual commands in the query language or within the design of a graphical user interface (GUI). A GUI will probably have at least three sub-windows: (i) a text window for displaying the textual representation of a collection of objects, containing for each object its alphanumeric attributes, (ii) a graphics window containing the overlay of the graphical representations of spatial attributes of several object classes or query results, and (iii) a text window for entering queries and perhaps displaying system messages. One possible design is shown in [EgF88]. Some systems implement a text-graphic interaction: clicking at an object representation in the text or graphic window selects and highlights the object representations in both windows (e.g. [ViO92]).

Egenhofer [Eg94] suggests to view a query as consisting of three parts:

- Describing the set of objects to be retrieved, as in traditional querying,
- Partitioning the query result into subsets to be displayed in different formats by a number of display queries,
- Describing for each subset how to render its spatial attributes.

For part (i), the language SQL, extended by spatial types and operations is used in [Eg94]. For parts (ii) and (iii) a special graphical presentation language (GPL) [Eg91a] is introduced which allows to give specifications for most of the requirements listed above.

7.3 Integrating Geometry into a Query Language

Integrating geometry into a query language has the following three main aspects:

(i) Denoting SDT values as constants in a query and graphical input of such constants.
(ii) Expressing the four classes of fundamental operations (Section 3.1) for an embedded spatial algebra.
(iii) Describing the presentation of results.

Denoting SDT values/graphical input. In traditional query languages, constants in queries (needed in particular to formulate selection conditions, e.g. name = "Smith") belong to an alphanumeric data type and are therefore textually representable, that is, can simply be entered through the keyboard. This is not feasible for SDT constants. Such a constant may be entered through a graphical input device or it could also have been computed in a previous query, for example, by extracting the attribute value of some object from the database. In Section 3.1 we have assumed that it is possible to introduce names for such values (Bavaria, Window, Hagen). This is not the case in classical relational query languages. In the geo-relational algebra [Güt88] atomic values are "first class citizens", so one can introduce a named REGION value Bavaria as follows:

states extract[sname = "Bavaria"; area] {Bavaria}

Object-oriented query languages usually allow one to identify one single object; one can then denote any attribute value (and therefore, an SDT value) by dot notation (e.g. determine an object "Bavaria" and then refer to "Bavaria.area"). If it is possible to denote such values, then one can nicely decouple graphical input and querying; the user interface allows one to draw the value and assign a name to it which can then be used in queries. If it is not possible, then a suggested technique [ChF80, Fra82, Eg94], is to use a special keyword within a query such as PICK; parsing the query will lead to an interaction that allows the user to graphically enter the value, for example:

SELECT sname FROM cities WHERE center inside PICK

Expressing the four classes of fundamental operations. Obviously, there is no problem at all to express spatial selection or spatial join since selection and join are provided by all query languages. Spatial function application, although not possible in classical relational algebra, is also in practice provided by query languages (in SQL by allowing expressions in the SELECT clause). Hence we can express the example queries of Section 3.1 as well in SQL or other languages (assuming denoting constants is possible):

SELECT * FROM rivers WHERE route intersects Window

SELECT cname, sname FROM cities, states WHERE center inside area

SELECT rname, intersection(route, Bavaria), length(intersection(route, Bavaria))
FROM rivers
WHERE route intersects Bavaria

In contrast, the expression of other set operations of a spatial algebra does not fit into the select ... from ... where (SFW) paradigm since these are algebra operations at the same level as projection, cartesian product, and selection captured by SFW. Some syntactic facilities required in a query language to accomodate a spatial algebra completely are described in [GütS93b] where a general "object model interface" is described.

Describing the presentation of results. It is arguable whether this should be part of a query language, be described by a separate language, or be defined by user interface manipulation. An interesting observation is that a presentation language also needs some embedded general querying capabilities, to determine subsets of answers to be shown in specific formats [Eg94, Eg91a].

Proposals for spatial query languages have been described, for example, in [ChF80, Fra82, LiN87, KePI87, HeLS88, JoC88, RoFS88, Güt88, ScV89, OoSM89, SvH91, Eg94]. Problems with SQL-based extensions are discussed in [Eg92]. Other directions in spatial querying include a deductive database approach [AbWP93] or visual querying [MaP90, Me92], that is, drawing a sketch of the spatial situations to be retrieved.

8. Tools for Spatial DBMS Implementation: Data Structures and Algorithms

We now consider system implementation bottom-up. In this section we first describe data structures and algorithms that can be used as tools or building blocks within different system architectures. System architectures themselves are discussed in the next section. The general problem to be solved is implementation of a spatial algebra in such a way that it can be integrated into a database system's query processing. This means, first of all, that we have to provide representations for the algebra's types as well as algorithms/procedures for its operations. However, it does not suffice just to implement atomic operations efficiently such as a test whether two regions intersect. It is also necessary to consider the use of such predicates within set-oriented query processing, that is, when they occur within a spatial selection or a spatial join. Here spatial access methods and spatial join algorithms come into play. Last not least, other set operations of a spatial algebra need their special implementations. In the following subsections we discuss representation of spatial data types and implementation of atomic operations, spatial indexing to support spatial selection, and support of spatial join.

8.1 Representing SDT Values and Implementing Atomic SDT Operations

The representation of a value of a spatial data type, e.g. a region, has to be simultaneously compatible with two different views, namely, the view of the database system, and the view of the spatial algebra. From the DBMS perspective, the representation

- is the same as that of attribute values of other types with respect to generic operations,
- can have varying and possibly very large size,
- resides permanently on disk and is stored in one page or a set of pages,
- can efficiently be loaded into main memory, where it is given as a value of some variable (typically, a pointer variable) to the procedures implementing operations of the spatial algebra,
- offers a number of type-specific implementations of generic operations needed by the DBMS.

From the point of view of the spatial algebra implementation which is done in some programming language, most likely the DBMS implementation language, the representation

- is a value of some programming language data type, e.g. region,
-
  is some arbitrary data structure which is possibly quite complex,
- supports efficient computational geometry algorithms for spatial algebra operations,
- is not geared only to one particular algorithm but is balanced to support many operations well enough.

To fulfill the requirements of the DBMS, the representation must be a paged data structure compatible with the DBMS support for long fields or large attribute values. To support efficient loading and storing on disk, it should consist of a single contiguous byte block as long as it is small enough to fit into one page. Otherwise it can be a large byte block cut into page sized pieces. The DBMS may then either allocate enough internal space to hold the whole value (and map pages into the right positions of this buffer) or implement a more complex paging strategy to access the value. For the case that a value representation happens to be large, a good strategy is to split it into a small info part, which will contain often used summary information about the value, and an exact geometry part, representing e.g. the long sequence of vertices, so that it is possible to load only the info part into a DBMS buffer. For example, the info part might be contained in the DBMS object representation and contain a logical pointer to a separate page sequence holding the exact geometry part. The generic operations needed by the DBMS may concern, for example, transforming from/to a textual or graphic representation for input/output at the user interface, or transforming from/to an ASCII format for bulk loading or external data exchange. More specifically, for spatial data types, generic approximations may be needed to interface with spatial access methods, for example, each data type must provide access to a bounding box (also called minimum bounding rectangle (MBR)).

From the spatial algebra and also the programming language point of view, the representation should be such that it is mapped by the compiler into a single or perhaps a few contiguous areas (to support the DBMS loading). For example, it can be defined as a pointer to a record with several fixed size components and a very large array (for the exact geometry) at the end; one can then dynamically allocate the right amount of space for a given value. Apart from that, the representation can support operations as follows:

- Plane sweep sequence. Very often, algorithms on the exact geometry use a plane-sweep. The sweep needs the components of the object (e.g. the vertices) in some fixed order, e.g. x-order. It is highly advantageous to store this order explicitly in the object so that not every sweep needs to sort vertices first.
- Approximations. The implementation of many operations starts with a rough test on an approximation of the object. Usually this is the bounding box, but there can also be other approximations. Hence these should be part of the representation.
- Stored unary function values. Some operations of the spatial algebra compute properties of a spatial value, e.g. the area or perimeter of a region. Since these can be expensive to compute, they may be computed once after creation of the value and then be stored with it.

The representation strategy described above does in fact assume a particular DBMS architecture, namely, that of an extensible DBMS. Hence some of the remarks may not be valid for an architecture which, for example, stores its SDT values separately in files, outside of the DBMS storage management. However, there seems to be growing agreement that the extensible approach is the right one as a basis for spatial database systems (e.g. [HaC91, ViO92, LaPV93]).

Issues of the representation of data type values in extensible DBMS ("abstract data type support") have been discussed, for example, in [StRG83, OsH86, Wilm88, Wo89, DrSW90]. The DASDBS Geo-Kernel [Wo89, DrSW90] makes somewhat special assumptions about the interface to a generic spatial access method by requiring that each data type must offer generic operations for clipping at a rectangle and composing two clipped pieces of an SDT value. The

Gral system [Güt89, BeG92] is an example of a system implementing the strategy described above.

Concerning the implementation of SDT operations, some important ideas such as prechecking onapproximations, looking up stored function values, and using plane-sweep, have already been mentioned. Generally, efficient algorithms from computational geometry should be used [PrS85, Me84]. For some operations, a simple scan of the vertices or edges is sufficient (e.g. to compute the perimeter or area of a region, or the center of a set of points). For more complex questions, most often plane-sweep is the appropriate technique (e.g. to compute the intersection of two polygons).

The implementation of many operations is simplified, if the spatial algebra has a discrete basis , for example, is realm-based. Basically, this means that in query processing there are never any new intersection points computed; all intersection points of SDT values over the realm are known within the realm and occur in both objects. For example, to compute the intersection of two lines values (which is a points value) in the ROSE algebra (see Section 2.3) it is sufficient to do a parallel scan on the two values' halfsegment sequences. (Each line segment occurring within a lines value is represented twice, once for the left end point, and once for the right end point – so each halfsegment has a dominating point. The halfsegment sequence is ordered xy-lexicographically by dominating points. Hence a parallel scan will determine the intersection points in linear time.) Without the realm basis, a much more complex plane-sweep algorithm is needed. Plane-sweep algorithms are also simplified with a realm-basis, because the sweep-event structure [NiP82] can now be a static data structure, since no new intersection points are discovered during the sweep. Such techniques are used in the implementation of the ROSE algebra [Ri94].

8.2 Spatial Indexing – Supporting Spatial Selection

The main purpose of spatial indexing is to support spatial selection, that is, to retrieve from a large set of spatial objects (objects with an SDT attribute) those in some particular relationship with a query SDT value. A spatial indexing method organizes space and the objects in it in some way so that only parts of the space and a subset of the objects need to be considered to answer such a query. There are two ways to provide spatial indexing: (i) dedicated external spatial data structures are added to the system, offering for spatial attributes what e.g. a B-tree does for standard attributes, and (ii) spatial objects are mapped into a one-dimensional space so that they can be stored within a standard one-dimensional index such as a B-tree. Apart from spatial selection, spatial indexing supports also other operations such as spatial join, finding the object closest to a query value, etc.

A fundamental idea also for spatial indexing, and in fact, for all spatial query processing, is the use of approximations. This means that the index structure manages an object in terms of one or more spatial keys which are much simpler geometric objects than the SDT value itself. One can distinguish continuous or grid approximations. A continuous approximation is based on the coordinates of the SDT value itself. The prime example is the bounding box (the smallest axis-parallel rectangle enclosing the SDT value). For grid approximations, space is divided into cells by a regular grid and the SDT value is represented by the set of cells that it intersects. Figure 5 illustrates the two kinds of approximations. The use of approximations leads to a filter and refine strategy for query processing [OrM88, Fra81]: First, based on the approximations, a filtering step is executed which returns a set of candidates which is a superset of the objects fulfilling a predicate. Second, for each candidate (or pair of candidates in case of spatial join) in a refinement step the exact geometry is checked. This strategy has more recently been extended to include a second filtering step where more precise approximations of the candidate objects are checked [BrKS93a].

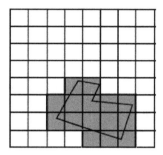

Figure 5: Bounding box and grid approximations of an SDT value

Due to the use of bounding boxes, most spatial data structures are designed to store either a set of points (for point values) or a set of rectangles (for line or region values). The operations offered by such a structure are insert, delete, and member (find a stored rectangle or point) to manage the set as such. Apart from that, one or more query operations are supported. For stored points, some important types of queries are:

- Range query: Find all points within a query rectangle.
- Nearest neighbour: Find the point closest to a query point.
- Distance scan: Enumerate points in increasing distance from a query point.

For rectangles:
- Intersection query: Find all rectangles intersecting a query rectangle.
- Containment query: Find all rectangles completely within a query rectangle.

A spatial index structure organizes objects within a set of buckets (which normally correspond to pages of secondary memory – some special approaches use varying size buckets with many pages [DrS93]). Each bucket has an associated bucket region – a part of space containing all objects stored in the bucket. Bucket regions are usually rectangles. For point data structures, these regions are normally disjoint and partition the space so that each point belongs into precisely one bucket. For some rectangle data structures, bucket regions may overlap. Figure 6 shows a partition where each bucket can hold up to 3 points.

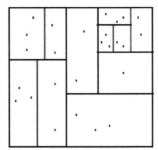

Figure 6: A kd-tree partitioning of a 2d-space

Like index structures for standard attributes, the structure can be clustering or a secondary index. A clustering index stores the actual spatial objects. An entry in a secondary index is just a spatial key (e.g. point or rectangle) together with a logical pointer to the object in the database. In the following three subsections we first consider one-dimensional embeddings that allow one to use standard index structures such as a B-tree. We then discuss dedicated spatial data structures for points and for rectangles.

8.2.1 One-Dimensional Embedding of Grid Approximations

The basic idea for this is to (i) find a linear order for the cells of the grid such that cells close together in space are also (as far as possible) close to each other in the linear order, and (ii) to define this order recursively for a grid that is obtained by a hierarchical subdivision of space.

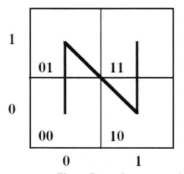
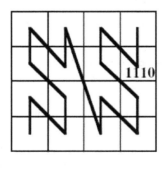

Figure 7: z-order enumeration of cells of a hierarchical partition

Figure 7 shows the most popular such order proposed by Morton [Mo66] as bit interleaving and later rediscovered several times (e.g. [AbS83, Ga82]). Orenstein [Or86] used it as a general basis for query processing in the PROBE system [OrM88] and introduced the name z-order for it. In Figure 7, the left diagram shows the ordering imposed on the 4 quadrants of the top level of a regular hierarchical partition. On the right side, this is continued to the next level: within each quadrant, cells are connected in z-order and then the groups of cells of the four quadrants are again connected in z-order. Each cell at each level of the hierarchy has an associated bit string whose length corresponds to the level the cell belongs to. For example, the top right cell in the left diagram has bit string 11, on the right side cell 1110 is shown. The bit string 1110 is obtained by choosing 11 at the top level and then 10 within the top level quadrant, one can also think of it as being composed of a 11 x-coordinate (used for the first and third bit) and a 10 y-coordinate (used for the second and fourth bit) which has led to the name bit interleaving. The order which is so imposed on all cells of a hierarchical subdivision is given by the lexicographical order of the bit strings.

Any shape (set of cells) over the grid can now be decomposed into a minimal number of cells at different levels, using always the highest possible level. It can therefore be represented by a set of bit strings (see Figure 8), called z-elements by Orenstein.

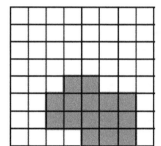 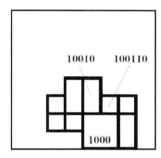

Figure 8: A set of z-elements approximating an SDT value

For a given spatial object, one can therefore use its corresponding set of z-elements as a set of spatial keys. To build an index for a set of objects, one can just form the union of all these spatial keys and put them in lexicographical order into a B-tree. Because of the proximity-preserving property of this embedding, various types of queries can now be answered relatively efficiently through B-tree access. For example, to answer a containment or range query with a rectangle r, this rectangle is itself decomposed into a number of z-elements. For each z-element, one portion of the leaf sequence of the B-tree is scanned containing all entries having that z-element as a prefix. This returns a set of candidates which can then be checked in the refine step whether containment is actually true.

8.2.2 Spatial Index Structures for Points

Data structures for representing points in an k-dimensional space have a much longer tradition than spatial database systems. This is, because a tuple consisting of n attributes, $t = (x1, ..., xk)$, can be viewed as a point in k dimensions, and therefore such data structures can be used to support multi-attribute retrieval. On the other hand, they can as well store points with a geometrical interpretation. Two well-known representatives of such data structures are the grid file [NiHS84] and the kd-tree [Be75]. The latter one is an internal data structure but has also been used as a basis for external index structures.

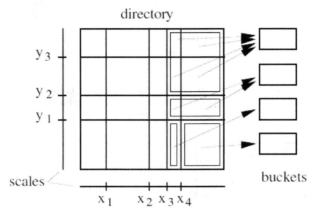

Figure 9: Structure of the grid file

The grid file (Figure 9) partitions the data space by an irregular grid into cells. Characteristic for this partition is that split lines extend through the whole space. The split line positions are kept in scales, using one scale per dimension. The directory is an k-dimensional array whose entries are logical pointers to buckets. Each cell of the data space corresponds to one element of the directory array, and all points lying within a cell are stored in the bucket pointed to by the corresponding directory entry. Several cells may be mapped into the same bucket so that bucket regions in general consist of more than one cell, as shown in Figure 9.

The scales are relatively small structures and can be kept in memory; the directory resides in a set of pages on disk. To find the bucket containing a particular point, one would determine with the help of the scales the address of the page containing the directory entry for the cell containg it. The second page access retrieves already this bucket. Range queries can be answered by determining from the directory the set of buckets containing cells intersected by the query rectangle, and then examining the points in these buckets. For the treatment of overflows or underflows of buckets see [NiHS84].

The kd-tree is a binary tree where each internal node contains a key drawn from one of the k dimensions; leaves contain the points to be stored. The key in the root node (at level 0, counting from top to bottom) divides the data space with respect to dimension 0, the keys in its sons, at level 1, divide the two subspaces with respect to dimension 1, and so forth, up to dimension k-1, after which cycling through the dimensions restarts. Figure 6 shows a kd-tree partitioning of the data space. For the original kd-tree, the recursive splitting of space stops when each cell contains only a single point. This has been transformed to an external data structure by letting each cell of the partition correspond to a bucket and by also paging the binary tree itself, in the

KDB-tree [Ro81] which is also a generalization of the B-tree (all leaves are at the same level). Another variant is the LSD-tree [HeSW89] which abandons the strict cycling through the dimensions and makes it possible to choose the dimension for splitting based on local criteria (therefore called local split decision tree). The second important aspect of the LSD-tree is a clever paging algorithm which keeps the external path length balanced even for very unbalanced binary trees. This allows the LSD-tree to deal rather well with skewed distributions of points which arise in particular when extended spatial objects (k-dimensional boxes, rectangles) are mapped into points through the transformation approach (see below). – Other point data structures are, for example, EXCELL [Ta82], the buddy hash tree [SeK90], the BANG file [Fr87], or the hB-tree [LoS89].

8.2.3 Spatial Index Structures for Rectangles

The management of rectangles in external data structures is more difficult than that of points because rectangles, unlike points, generally do not fall into a unique cell of a partition, but intersect partition boundaries. There are three solutions for this problem:

- The transformation approach: Instead of k-dimensional rectangles, we store 2k-dimensional points, using a point data structure.
- Overlapping regions: Partitioning space is abandoned; bucket regions may overlap.
- Clipping: We keep partitioning space; if a rectangle intersects partition boundaries it is clipped into several pieces and represented within each cell that it intersects.

The transformation approach. A rectangle, represented by four coordinates (xleft, xright, ybottom, ytop), can be regarded as a point in four dimensions. The various types of queries then map to regions of the 4d-space. This approach is usually illustrated by the case of intervals mapped into 2d-space .

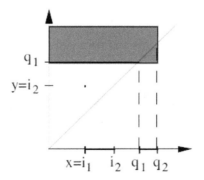

Figure 10: The transformation approach, mapping intervals into 2d-points

In Figure 10, the interval to be stored, $i = (i1, i2)$, is mapped into a point (x, y). An intersection query with an interval $q = (q1, q2)$ translates to a condition: Find all points (x', y') such that $x' <$

q2 and q1 < y'. Hence all intervals intersecting q must lie as points in the shaded area shown in Figure 10. The transformation approach [Hi85, SeK88], here shown with the corner representation, generally leads to rather skewed distributions of points. For example, all points fall into the area above the diagonal x = y. If all intervals are small, all corresponding points lie very close to this diagonal. It is also possible to use a center representation (using center and length of an interval) but then the query regions become cone-shaped which does not fit so well with rectangular partitions of the point set. The LSD-tree point data structure was designed particularly with the goal to be able to adapt to such skewed distributions [HeSW89]. A recent discussion of the transformation approach and a comparison to methods storing rectangles directly can be found in [PaST93].

Overlapping regions. The prime example of a structure using overlapping bucket regions is the R-tree [Gu84], illustrated in Figure 11.

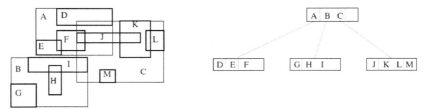

Figure 11: A set of rectangles represented by an R-tree

It is a multiway tree, like the B-tree, and stores in each node a set of rectangles. For the leaves, these are the rectangles of the set R to be represented. For an internal node, each rectangle is associated with a pointer to a son p and represents the bucket region of p which is the bounding box of all rectangles represented within p. For example, in Figure 11 the root node contains a rectangle A which is the bounding box of the rectangles D, E, and F stored in the son associated with A. Rectangles may overlap; hence, a rectangle can intersect several bucket regions but will be represented only in one of them. An advantage is that a spatial object can be kept in just one bucket. A problem is that search needs now to branch and follow several paths whenever one is interested in a region lying in the overlap of two son regions. To keep search efficient, it is crucial to minimize the overlap of node regions. This is determined by the split strategy on overflow. Several strategies based on different heuristics have been studied in [Gu84, Gr89, Beck90]; the one proposed in [Beck90], called R*-tree, appeared to perform best in experiments. Clipping. A variant of the R-tree, called R+-tree, was proposed by [SeRF87, FaSR87] and used in the PSQL database system [RoFS88]. It avoids overlapping regions associated with buckets or inter-nal nodes of the same level completely by clipping data rectangles, if necessary.

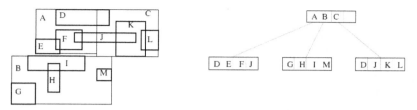

Figure 12: A set of rectangles represented by an R+-tree

In Figure 12, an R+-tree is shown for the same set of data rectangles as in Figure 11. Here the rectangles A, B, and C in the root are chosen a bit differently to keep them, and therefore the three sons' bucket regions, disjoint. Now it is necessary to clip rectangles D and J so that each of them is represented in two buckets. Experimental comparisons of spatial index structures including R-tree variants can be found in [Gr89, SmG90, Beck90]. There has been a tremendous amount of work on spatial index structures and it is not possible in this survey to cover it completely. Other directions include quadtree variants (surveyed in [Sa90]) which are closely related to the grid approximation schemes of Section 4.2.1, or cell trees [Gün88, GünB89] which do not store rectangles but work with polygonal subdivisions of the plane directly. An excellent survey of spatial index structures can be found in [Wi91]. The paper by Lin, Jagadish, and Faloutsos in this special issue introduces the TV-tree, a data structure for indexing sets of points in a high-dimensional space, which is somewhat similar to an R-tree. It is a good example for the design and analysis techniques needed in the development of spatial index structures as described in this section.

It should be clear now that spatial index structures offering a few fundamental query operations can support through the filter and refine strategy selection with many different spatial predicates. For example, a query for all regions in a partition adjacent to a given region can be answered by checking candidates from an intersection query; to find all regions within a certain distance from a query point one can also find candidates by an intersection query using a suitable square around the point.

The filter and refine strategy has been extended in [BrKS93a] to include a second filter step with finer approximations than the bounding box; they compared, for example, bounding ellipses, convex hulls, and convex 5-corners. These are conservative approximations which means they include the actual SDT values. Better conservative approximations are able to exclude some false hits from further consideration. In the second filter step one can also use progressive approximations, which are contained in the actual SDT value, such as a maximum enclosed circle or a maximum enclosed rectangle [Brin94]. These allow one to identify hits; if two progressive approximations intersect, their SDT values are guaranteed to intersect. The goal is always to avoid as far as possible the expensive loading and comparison of the exact geometries. It has also been suggested to decompose very large SDT values into several components so that checking the exact geometry can for most queries be restricted to one of the components [KrHS91].

51

8.3 Supporting Spatial Join

Spatial join, as described in Section 3.1, determines for two sets of spatial objects all objects in a relationship described by a spatial predicate. Classical join methods such as hash join or sort/merge join are not applicable. Filtering the cartesian product is possible but too expensive. Central ideas for computing spatial joins are, again, the filter and refine strategy, and the use of spatial index structures. One can classify proposed strategies along the following criteria:

- Grid approximation/bounding box
- None/one/both operands are represented in a spatial index structure. For grid approximations, and for an overlap predicate, Orenstein [Or86, OrM88] described join algorithms to determine pairs of candidates. Essentially a parallel scan of the two sets of z-elements corresponding to the two sets of spatial objects is performed, similar to a merge join for a "£" predicate.

Note that overlay, a particularly important operations for GIS, is a special case [Or91]. A general problem with grid approximations is that choosing a too fine grid leads to inefficiency because too many z-elements per object are created whereas a too rough grid may deliver too many "false hits" in a spatial join [Or89].

If the filter step is based on the use of bounding boxes, then the problem is to determine for two sets of rectangles R, S, all pairs (r, s), r $\hat{I}$ R, s $\hat{I}$ S, such that r intersects s. If none of the operands is represented in a spatial index, a good technique is to use a rectangle intersection algorithm from computational geometry which solves precisely this problem. Such an algorithm, called bb_join, has been used in the Gral system [Güt89, BeG92]. The basis is an external divide-and-conquer algorithm [BeG92, GütS87], somewhat similar to external merge sorting. Note that even when base object sets are represented in a spatial index, such a method is needed in query processing, for example, when the two operand sets have been determined through other indexes, or are themselves the result of geometric set operations. This has also been emphasized by [LoR94] who suggest to build an index for one of the operands on the fly and describe a new tree structure, seeded trees, particularly suitable for this.

If one operand is represented in a spatial index, then an index join or repeated search join can be used [BeG92, LoR94]. This is a classical technique, usually used with a B-tree index, which can equally well be applied to spatial index structures. Hence, if the "inner" operand is represented in an index supporting rectangle intersection queries, one can scan the "outer" operand set; for each object, the bounding box of its SDT attribute is used as a search argument on the index. As a result one obtains again a set of candidate pairs with intersecting rectangles. Repeated search join is especially efficient if the outer set is not too big (for example, is the result of a selection from a large set). If both sets are large, bb_join may win. Such choices have to be made by the query optimizer.

Recent research into spatial join methods has focused on the case that both operands have a spatial index. The basic idea is then to perform a somehow synchronized traversal of the two index structures so that pairs of cells of their respective partitions covering the same part of space are encountered together. A parallel traversal of two grid files has been examined in

52

[Ro91, BeHF93], of R-trees in [BrKS93b]. Günther [Gün93] studies traversal of generalization trees which can represent nested polygonal partitions directly but can also be viewed as a generalization of R-trees, for example. He also derives cost formulas for several distributions and compares the cost of nested loop join (i.e. filtering the cartesian product), tree traversal, and use of join indices.

The use of join indices [Va87] has also been applied to spatial joins. A join index contains all pairs of object identifiers for objects from two sets in a given relationship of interest. Rotem [Ro91] describes the computation of a join index from two grid files which combines pairs of points within distance e from each other, and also the maintenance of such an index under grid file reorganizations. A problem is that the index is based on some fixed distance and does not support well queries with other distances. In [LuH92] some variations are suggested to accomodate different distances. Unfortunately, if all distances are to be supported, the join index will have a quadratic number of entries which is not feasible for large sets of objects.

After the filter step, similar as for spatial selection, one may insert a second filter step with better approximations to determine hits and exclude false hits from further checking [Brin94].

9. System Architecture

9.1 Requirements

At the level of system architecture, the problem is to integrate the tools described in Section 4 for the support of spatial data types – and even more than that. In principle, the following extensions to a standard architecture need to be accomodated:

- representations for the data types of a spatial algebra,
- procedures for the atomic operations,
- spatial index structures,
- access operations for spatial indices,
- filter and refine techniques,
- spatial join algorithms,
- cost functions for all these operations,
- statistics for estimating selectivity of spatial selection and spatial join,
- extensions of the optimizer to map queries into the specialized query processing methods,
- spatial data types and operations within data definition and query language,
- user interface extensions to handle graphical representation and input of SDT values.

In our view, the only clean way to accomodate these extensions is an integrated architecture based on the use of an extensible DBMS. Nevertheless, GIS have been constructed before extensible DBMS technology was available, and we shall first review previous approaches to GIS architecture.

9.2 GIS Architectures – Using a Closed DBMS

The first generation of GIS was built directly on top of file systems and did not offer the benefits of DBMS such as high-level data definition, flexible querying, transaction management, etc. They are not further discussed here. When DBMS technology and in particular, relational systems, became available, attempts were made to use them as a basis. The two main approaches are layered architecture and dual architecture (following the terminology of [ViO92], see also [LaPV93]).

Layered architecture. Here spatial functionality is implemented on top of a given DBMS, often a commercially available relational system, as shown in Figure 13.

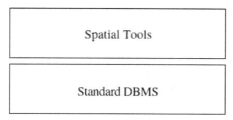

Figure 13: Layered architecture

For the representation of SDT values, there are two possible strategies. The first, used in early work [BeS77, ChF80], is to let each tuple represent the coordinates of one point or line segment and to break the SDT value into pieces (e.g. represent a polygon as a subset of a line segment relation). The disadvantage is that for the implementation of SDT operations in the top layer, the SDT values have first to be reconstructed which is far too expensive. The second possibility is to represent SDT values in "long fields" of the DBMS (e.g. GEOVIEW [WaH87], SIRO-DBMS [Ab89]). This is better than breaking SDT values into pieces; it is still problematic because the DBMS handles the geometries only in the form of uninterpreted byte strings; evaluation of any predicate or operation on an exact geometry can only be done in the top layer. Some limited form of spatial indexing can be provided by maintaining sets of z-elements (see Section 4.2.1) for the geometries in special relations which in turn can be indexed through a B-tree.

Dual Architecture. Here a top layer integrates two rather independent subsystems: the DBMS which handles non-spatial data, and a spatial subsystem storing and manipulating geometries (Figure 14).

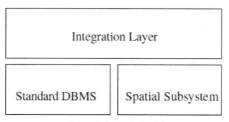

Figure 14: Dual Architecture

With this approach, the representation of each spatial object (object with an SDT attribute) is broken into two pieces. The first part contains the non-spatial attributes and is stored in the DBMS. The second part is the spatial attribute and is kept in data structures implemented directly on top of the file system. The two pieces are connected by logical pointers. This approach is followed by most commercial GIS (e.g. ARC/INFO [Mo89], SICAD [Sc85]) as well as some research prototypes (e.g. [OoSM89]).

An advantage is that one is free to use adequate representations of SDT values as well as efficient data structures and algorithms for indexing and query processing within the spatial subsystem. For example, in [OoSM89] a spatial kd-tree [OoMS87] is used as an index structure. A problem is that a query now has to be decomposed into a non-spatial part and a spatial part, to be handled by the DBMS and the spatial subsystem, respectively. This complicates query processing and leads to overhead. Perhaps the main problem is that no global query optimization is possible. For example, if a query can be processed by either using an index on a standard attribute or one on a spatial attribute, the integration layer cannot compare the two plans since estimated costs from the standard DBMS are not available. Query optimization under the dual architecture has been studied in [OoSM89].

A different view of a dual architecture is taken in [ArS91a]. Again, spatial and non-spatial parts of an object are stored in separate structures and linked by logical pointers. However, the intention is not to use a standard DBMS, but to be able to use specialized storage structures for the geometries, and to implement the concept within one new database system. The consequences of dealing in query processing with relations represented by two separate storage structures are studied in [ArS91b]. The PSQL system [RoFS88] has a similar dual architecture within an extended relational prototype.

9.3 Integrated Spatial DBMS Architecture – Using an Extensible DBMS

Research into extensible database systems (e.g. POSTGRES [StR86], Probe [Daya87], EXODUS [GrD87], GENESIS [Bato88], Starburst [Haas89], Gral [Güt89], Sabrina [Gard89], DASDBS [Sche90]) was aimed at making precisely the kinds of extensions required in Section 5.1 possible. The use of an extensible system leads to an integrated architecture which takes the following view:

- There is no difference in principle between a "standard" data type such as STRING and a spatial data type such as REGION. This includes operations; for example, there is no difference in principle between concatenating two strings or forming the intersection of two regions. System architecture should treat them in the same way.
- There is no difference in principle between a clustering or secondary index for standard attributes (e.g. a B-tree) and for spatial attributes (e.g. an R-tree).
- Similarly, a sort/merge join, and a bounding-box join, are basically the same.
- The mechanisms for query optimization should not distinguish spatial or other operations (of course, differences may be reflected in the cost functions).

Such an integrated architecture can in principle also be obtained by implementing a new database system from scratch or making appropriate extensions to the code of a given DBMS. Using an extensible DBMS just vastly reduces the effort. Furthermore, a spatial DBMS based on an extensible DBMS is open for extensions, and so allows one to add missing functionality, at any time. This is particularly important because it is not known how to determine a closed, complete set of operations of a spatial algebra.

The architecture of an extensible DBMS essentially offers slots and registration facilities for all (or most of) the kinds of extensions listed in Section 5.1. An attempt to illustrate this is given in Figure 15 where spatial components are shaded and only a few of the places for extension are shown.

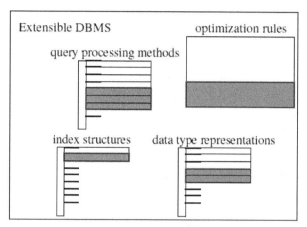

Figure 15: Integrated, extensible architecture

Several spatial DBMS prototypes based on extensible systems have been built, examples are Probe [Or86, OrM88], the DASDBS GEO-Kernel [Sche90, Wo89], and Gral [Güt89, BeG92]. Possible uses of extensibility, in particular in the context of the Starburst system, for spatial database applications have been discussed in [HaC91]. More recent prototypes are GEO++ [OoV91, ViO92] based on POSTGRES, and GéoSabrina [LaPV93] based on Sabrina.

In the Probe system [Or86, OrM88], spatial data types can be introduced as refinements (within an object-oriented class hierarchy) of a general POINT-SET data type. For all such types, the system provides built-in support in the form of approximate geometry processing. This means that SDT values are represented by sets of z-elements and that the filter step for spatial selections (that is, spatial indexing) and spatial joins is offered in the system kernel. Recall that this work was a major proponent of the filter and refine strategy for spatial query processing [OrM88].

Work in the DASDBS project [Sche90, Wo89] has focused on external data type (EDT) support and on interfacing to generic spatial access methods. The EDT concept is a variant of data type extensibility assuming that data structures for an EDT and procedures working on these data structures are probably not coded specifically for the DBMS but rather have existed in an application environment long before. The DBMS should be able to work with these given programming language representations by using appropriate conversion functions. This has recently been extended to let the DBMS cooperate with a "geometric computation service" (as an implementation of a spatial algebra) over a network within different run-time environments

[ScW93]. For spatial indexing, generic access methods partitioning the data space into cells such as the grid file or the R+-tree are assumed; to interface with such an access method, each SDT implementation has to offer a clip and a compose function to determine the piece of the geometry falling into one cell and to put pieces together again, respectively.

The Gral system [Güt89, BeG92] emphasizes many-sorted algebra as a formal basis for its extensible system architecture; it uses such algebras to describe application-specific query languages and query processing systems and provides a rule-based optimizer which transforms a query algebra expression to an executable expression by applying transformation rules. For spatial indexing, LSD-trees (see Section 4.2.2) are available; spatial joins are supported by repeated search on LSD-trees or a bounding-box-join algorithm (Section 4.3). The bounding box is the generic interface between any spatial data type and access or join methods. The system treats spatial and non-spatial data quite uniformly; in [BeG92] completely integrated query optimization and query processing are shown. It is also demonstrated there how filter and refine techniques are actually implemented in the optimizer.

Note that extensibility of a system architecture is rather orthogonal to the data model implemented by that architecture. For example, Probe offers an object-oriented or functional data model, DASDBS a nested relational model, and POSTGRES, Starburst and Gral extended relational models. Object-oriented systems have been considered as an implementation platform (e.g. [Davi93]). Such systems are extensible at the data type level. However, they generally lack extensibility at the levels of index structures, query processing methods (e.g. join algorithms), or query optimization which is crucial for spatial DBMS implementation. Experiments with an object-oriented system and some of the arising problems have been described in [ScV92].

10 Conclusions / Future Research

10.1 RESEARCH NEEDS

Spatial databases are being used for an increasing number of new applications, such as Intelligent Transportation Systems, NASA's Earth Observation System, Multimedia Information Systems (MMIS) and Data Warehouses. This section lists representative research needs.

Space Taxonomy

Many spatial applications manipulate continuous spaces of different scales and with different levels of discretization. A sequence of operations on discretized data can lead to growing errors similar to the ones introduced by finiteprecision arithmetic on numbers. There are preliminary results on the use of discrete basis and bounding errors with peg-board semantics. Another related problem concerns interpolation to estimate the continuous field from a discretization. Negative spatial autocorrelation makes interpolation error-prone. Further work is needed on a framework to formalize the discretization process, its associated errors, and on interpolation.

Spatial Data Model

Spatial data models have been developed for topological, metric and coordinative Euclidean space. The OGIS specification alluded to is confined to topological operators, and more work is needed to incorporate relationships which involve directional and metric properties. In addition, there has been very little work toward developing data models, data types (e.g., node, edge, path), and a kernel set of operations (e.g.,get-successors, shortest path) for network space, despite their critical role in applications like transportation and utility management (telephone, gas, electric). Similarly, there is a need for developing the field data model toward a field-based query language. Operations on fields will be needed to help derive new information such as land-cover classification; the fields involved include temperature, texture, and water content, and are obtained through imaging in different bands such as infrared, visible bands, or microwave.

Spatial Query Processing

Many open research areas exist at the logical level of query processing, including query-cost modeling and strategies for nearest neighbor, bulk loading as well as queries related to fields and networks. Cost models are used to rank and select the promising processing strategies, given a spatial query and a spatial data set. Traditional cost models may not be accurate in estimating the cost of strategies for spatial operations, due to the distance metric as well as the semantic gap between relational operators and spatial operation. Cost models are needed to estimate the selectivity of spatial search and join operations toward comparison of execution-costs of alternative processing strategies for spatial operations during query optimization. Preliminary work in the context of the R-tree, tree-matching join, and fractal-models is promising, but more work is needed. Similarly, common strategies employed in traditional databases for the logical transformation step in query optimization may not be always applicable in the context of spatial databases. Let us assume that the Area () function is not precomputed and that its value is computed afresh every time it is invoked. A query tree generated for the query is show in fig. In the classical situation, the rule "select before join" would dictate that the Area() function be computed before the join predicate function, Distance(), the underlying assumption being that the computational cost of executing the select and join predicate are equivalent and negligible compared to the I/O cost of the operations.

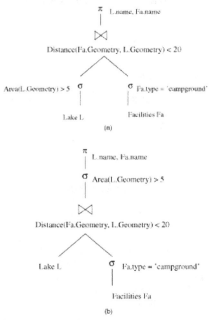

Fig.: (a) Area () before distance (); (b) Distance () before Area ().

In the spatial situation the relative cost per tuple of Area () and Distance () is an important factor in deciding the order of the operations. Depending upon the implementation of these two functions the optimal strategy may be to process the join before the select operation. Many processing strategies using the overlap predicate have been developed for range queries and spatial join queries. However, there is a need to develop and evaluate strategies for many other frequent queries . These include queries on objects using predicates other than overlap and queries on fields such as slope analysis as well as queries on networks such as the shortest path to a set of destinations. Bulk loading strategies for spatial data also need further study

Spatial File Organization and Indices: Physical Level

Many file organizations and indices with distance metrics have been developed for coordinative Euclidean space. However, little work has been done on file clustering and on indices for network spaces such as road maps and telephone networks. Further work is needed, both to characterize the access patterns of the graph algorithms that underlie network operations and to design access methods. The R-link tree [16] is among the few approaches available for concurrency control on the R-tree. New approaches for concurrency-control techniques are needed for other spatial indices. The data volume of emerging spatial applications such as NASA's EOS is among the highest of any database application. Sequoia 2000 [30] provides an approach toward tertiary storage files and indices. Other approaches for managing databases on tertiary storage need to be investigated.

DIFFICULT SPATIAL QUERIES FROM GIS

Buffer	Find the areas 500 ft. from power lines
Voronoize	Classify households as to which supermarket they are closest to
Neighborhood	Determine slope based on elevation
Network	Find the shortest path from the warehouse to all delivery stops
Allocation	Where is the best place to build a new restaurant
Transformation	Triangulate a layer based on elevation
Bulk Load	Load a spatial data file into the database
Raster ↔ Vector	Convert between raster and vector representations

Other

Other research needs include benchmarking, workflow modeling, and the visual presentation of results. The Sequoia 2000 benchmark characterizes the data and queries in Earth Science applications. The performance of loading data, raster queries, spatial selection, spatial joins, and recursion is addressed in 11 benchmark queries. A few more are provided in the Paradise system. Similar benchmarks are needed to characterize the spatial data management needs of other applications such as GIS, DWH, and transportation. The workflow in some spatial applications such as GIS is based on manipulating layers to produce new, derived layers. Typically, the layers are combined in a tree-based manner, starting with a large number of source layers and producing new layers until a final result layer is produced. Information about dependence among layers is useful for change propagation if the source layers are modified.

Spatial databases may require a different type of concurrency support than is needed by traditional databases. For example, transactions in traditional systems tend to be short (on the order of seconds). However, in spatial databases, these transactions can last up to a couple of hours for editing and browsing. Similarly, recovery and backup issues may also change, as the spatial objects tend be large (a few megabytes) when compared to their counterparts in traditional systems. There is a need to characterize the work flow of spatial applications.

Many spatial applications present results visually, in the form of maps which consist of graphic images, 3D displays, and animations. They also allow users to query the visual representation by pointing to the visual representation using devices like a mouse or a pen. Further work is needed to explore the impact of querying by pointing and visual presentation of results on database performance.

10.2 SUMMARY AND DISCUSSION

In this, we have presented the accomplishments and techniques which have emerged from the area of SDBMS. These include object-based data modeling, spatial data types, filter and refine techniques for query processing and spatial indexing. We have also identified areas where more research is needed. Some of these areas are spatial graphs, field based modeling, cost modeling and concurrency control, query processing techniques and discretization and propogation error.

Many of the spatial techniques highlighted in this survey are being used in an increasing number of applications such as GIS, CAD, and EOS. We believe that other emerging multidimensional applications such as multimedia information systems will use these methods to solve problems such as searching and indexing spatial content. We illustrate the possibilities in the context of multimedia information systems with text, audio and video data over the World Wide Web.

Multimedia data has a spatial content which can be queried using the same spatial operators that have become popular in geographic information systems. For example, the spatial operator inside of can be applied to text to locate sentences that contain the word "multimedia." Also, audio is often broken into channels with each channel containing input from a different source; for instance, trumpet, guitar, and voice. These channels are analogous to layers in GIS and can be manipulated similarly. A spatial join could determine all of the locations where the input from both piano and voice is over a certain decibel threshold.

A video database such as a movie server can take advantage of techniques developed for spatial databases. Consider the movie Toy Story: Each frame contains spatial content with objects interacting in directional relationships. For instance, Buzz Lightyear could be above the trees when he is flying, and frames in the movie could be queried based on those relationships. For example, if you cannot remember when in the movie an important event occurred, but you can remember that Buzz Lightyear was in front of a tree, you would be able to query the movie using that relationship to determine when in the movie that event took place. Such queries exploit the directional relationships inherent between all tangible objects.

10.3 Future Scope

The spatial databases of tomorrow will be shaped by two major influences - an improved ability to model reality and users demanding increased database access. Other potential influences such as price, platform, speed, storage capacity are considered here to be less important. This paper first outlines the limitations of current spatial databases and database design and then develops a conceptual framework for future design and access.

In the last decade spatial databases have continued to be designed and developed at a frenetic pace. This pace, in relative terms, is slowing - the quantum leap has yet to occur. Current spatial databases have a short history - not much more than 15 years. For the majority of that time they have evolved out of the proprietary pursuits of the leading vendors. Initially, Intergraph and ESRI (and others of o less endurance) dominated the field. Both companies responded to market forces and developed systems with simple database structures. The databases may have been flat files but mostly of the network and hierarchical structures. Advances have moved to relational and commercial databases. This has facilitated development and increased accessibility to data.

Spatial data remains separated from attribute data and there remain two distinct structures for representing spatial objects - vector or raster. Topological associations are now incorporated into the data structures but a true object paradigm has not become entrenched. This apparent reluctance to embrace the object oriented structures is intriguing given the early appearance for object oriented GISs. The acceptance of full topological and object structures were initially constrained by hardware and secondary storage. This is no longer the case but still there is no common use of object oriented database management systems (OODMSs).

There are considerable demands for improved spatial systems - where will they develop? This can partly be answered by understanding that current systems emerged from geography, geometrics' and mapping disciplines. These disciplines, it is contended, are responsible, rightly or wrongly, for the current spatial modeling paradigms. Will pressures from users and business imperatives direct development into areas such as, visualization, spatial analysis, data structures and databases or general functionality?

An improved spatial model

Where will it come from - what will its concepts be founded on - how will it be revolutionary? If it is possible to visually perceive the world as it surrounds us. Then it logically follows that it is possible to mentally store and recall these images. The human mind is capable of observing and understanding and even analyzing space and spatial objects.

Spatial databases will evolve to store and retrieve representations of space where these representations are more accurately (closer to the truth) aligned with the phenomena we perceive. It is tempting to delve into the workings of the mind, though this is resisted here and now. What is more important to realize is that current databases are constrained by their own pedigrees. In future, space and objects within it, collectively need to be represented differently in databases. Saying 'space and objects' is already pre-emptive. It is a breakdown of convenience; it may not be the best form. It is used here simply as a convenient way to explain an emerging concept.

It is held and developed here that spatial databases of the future will store space and objects as a whole - just as we perceive the world around us. Raster and vector will give way to space, object and knowledge. Representations will be born out of the concept that objects exist and have knowledge embedded in them - which they exist and behave in an observable and representative way. This may seem to be much the object oriented paradigm. It is more than that - much more if we are to succeed.

Figure I indicate the de-aggregation of reality and its re-aggregation into representations that may be stored in a database. The last two lines are a casual (or somewhat flippant) comment on possible scenarios. Any developments in spatial modeling must understand the primitive and substantive reason why user wants to model that environment - space.

$$\text{Object} = \text{Reality} - \text{Abstraction}$$

$$\text{Data} = \text{Object} + \text{Measurement}$$

$$\text{Information} = \text{Object} + \text{Data} + \text{Structure}$$

$$\text{Knowledge} = \text{Information} + \text{Use}$$

$$\text{Wisdom} = \text{Knowledge} + \text{Experience}$$

$$(\text{Hopelessness} = \text{Data} + \text{Experience})$$

$$(\text{Hopefulness} = \text{Objects} + \text{Knowledge})$$

Figure 1

It is intuitive that users collect and store spatial to either present it as is or to analyze it. The underlying reasons are possibly very complex and what's more possibly not all that relevant to this discussion. It more important to recognize that users are interested in understanding how components work together or the processes that has created and continue to modify a large continuous spatial phenomenon. A good example of the former is how people and albatross interact at a tourist attraction (reported elsewhere at this conference and Purvis et al., 1993) or why of two forest trees, why one is taller and healthier than the other. In the second case, is it possible to explain a geological fault, why a city exists, or what drives ocean upwelling and saline fronts.

From these isolated but typical examples it is not unrealistic to draw a conclusion that what is required is a model of reality, as intricate as possible, that relates a suitable number of its de-aggregated components, and allows for the analysis of these components. There is no use creating a wonderful model it the components are not identifiable or their interactions obliterated.

With this an explicit background it is possible to develop Figure 2. This figure shows the abstraction of reality data, entities and space. The implication is that initially then abstraction is to data as a consequence of the current field collection methods and techniques. When data are appropriately re-aggregated, eventually Space and Rules of existence are (re-)created. The choice or use of words here is somewhat arbitrary but nonetheless important. Object is not used so as to avoid confusion, but entity is unavoidable. The words used in Figure 2, may to some, abuse convention; the intention is that the higher one ascends in the text, the more holistic the model becomes.

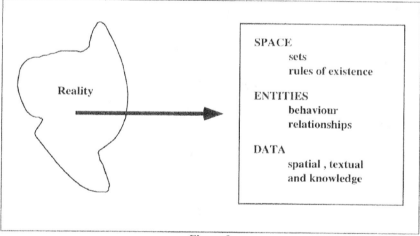

Figure 2

Current systems are at the entity (again, not to be confused with database terminology), behavior and relationships level. This may be manifest in relational databases, or object databases, either with full topological data structures.

The .Space stage with sets and rules may too he represented in a relational database. While that construct may be the same, the users' fundamental view of the data is different. What is seen is a set of spatial phenomena and a minimum set of rules that describe their classification. This could run in parallel with an object paradigm which stores these phenomena and their associated inheritance, behaviors etc.

If it is possible to store this structure then retrieval will be beneficial; Frawley et al. (1992) Described similar situations as the discovery of knowledge or knowledge extraction. They went on to say that what was really required from databases was, nontrivial extraction of implicit, previously unknown, and do potentially useful information from data, This in turn required a special classification technique for the phenomena being studied and means of retrieving or mining through the database.

To return to the human mind and perceptions of space for just a moment, The system description given above could be developed to be similar to the way we understand human discovery algorithms. We have a range of different methods For different types of problems. In fact we have different strategies for learning different problems, especially for classification, which apply a number of different methods to the same task and select rules from the best method (Brodley, 1993; Michalski and Tecuci, 1993).

These concepts can be considered to be closely related to the fields of rough sets and database knowledge discovery. The theory for the former was originally developed by Pawlak in the early 1980s. The primary methodological framework was to study classification problems with imprecise or incomplete information and the theory of rough sets was developed. This theory, to the best of the by author knowledge, has not been implemented and tested with spatial phenomena and knowledge extraction. There is considerable appeal to apply the theory to spatial data.

If the high level model shown in Figure 2 can be developed it may well be achieved using rough sets. The concept would be to develop a database of spatial phenomena, where the unique (or nearly unique) classification of the components is achieved with a minimum group of rules or class definitions. The key idea in the rough sets approach stems from the observation that imprecise representation data helps uncover data regularities. Any concern or belief here that we in fact know precisely the data and relationship should be discarded. The point of most geographic information systems is the analysis of the data to determine exactly that - what are the data regularities (and hence may be data irregularities)?

The theory of rough sets provides a collection of mathematical techniques to deal, with full mathematical rigour, with data classification problems (which once we would have called a layer or theme), particularly when data are noisy, incomplete or imprecise. Also rough set theory includes a formal model which defines knowledge as a family of indiscernibility relations which gives knowledge a clearly defined mathematical sense. This definition allows 'Knowledge' to be analyzed and manipulated using mathematical techniques.

Federated databases

Hand in glove with database developments is a concept federated databases. This is, in simple terms, the connection of several databases in such a way that the union is transparent.

Furthermore applications can access a data repository index which contains information on data, data structures, data use rules, data knowledge and other applications. The federation makes this possible from any application domain to any other using any data for any reason. A grand concept that is close to reality.

The concept of federated databases seems to be remote from the concept of rough sets. That may well not be the case. For, if there is a desire to extract knowledge from disparate data sets using the techniques described above, one of the imperatives will be easy access. It must be possible to trawl through several disparate (both in the contextual and geographic senses) databases in a way that does not inhibit the user of the search algorithms.

As an example considers a client - a private electricity company which relies on hydro electricity to meet peak load demands. Such a company will have to manage its resource, water at altitude and have appropriate models of supply and demand. These will be very variable in both time and location. Applications would include socio-demographics, climate and rainfall models, snow melts and load determination. it takes little further imagination to list the data sets required for these applications and that there will not be one single data source.

Future federated databases will provide an environment that execution of the models will be possible without detailed knowledge of where the data are or what structure they are stored in. It will even possible to remotely bill your account – of course.

11. References

1. [AbWP93] Abdelmoty, A.I., M.H. Williams, and N.W. Paton, Deduction and Deductive Databases for Geographic Data Handling. Proc. 3rd Intl. Symposium on Large Spatial Databases, Singapore, 1993, 443-464.

2. [Ab89] Abel, D.J., SIRO-DBMS: A Database Tool Kit for Geographical Information Systems. Intl. J. of Geographical Information Systems 3 (1989), 103-116.

3. [AbO93] Abel, D.J., and B.C. Ooi (eds.), Proceedings of the 3rd Intl. Symposium on Large Spatial Databases, Singapore. LNCS 692, Springer, 1993.

4. [AbS83] Abel, D.J., and J.L. Smith, A Data Structure and Algorithm Based on a Linear Key for a Rectangle Retrieval Problem. Computer Vision, Graphics, and Image Processing 24 (1983), 1-13.

5. [AbB88] Abiteboul, S., and C. Beeri, On the Power of Languages for the Manipulation of Complex Objects. Technical Report 846, INRIA (Paris), 1988.

6. [Ag87] Agrawal, R., ALPHA: An Extension of Relational Algebra to Express a Class of Recursive Queries. Proc. IEEE Data Engineering Conf. 1987, 580-590.

7. [ArS91a] Aref, W., and H. Samet, Extending a DBMS with Spatial Operations. Proc. 2nd Intl. Symposium on Large Spatial Databases, Zürich, 1991, 299-318.

8. [ArS91b] Aref, W., and H. Samet, Optimization Strategies for Spatial Query Processing. Proc. 17th Intl. Conf. on Very Large Data Bases, Barcelona, 1991, 81-90.

9. [Banc87] Bancilhon, F., T. Briggs, S. Khoshafian, and P. Valduriez, FAD, a Powerful and Simple Database Language. Proc. 13th Intl. Conf. on Very Large Data Bases, Brighton, 1987, 97-105.

10. [Bato88] Batory, D.S., J.R. Barnett, J.F. Garza, K.P. Smith, K. Tsukuda, B.C. Twichell, and T.E. Wise, GENESIS: An Extensible Database Management System. IEEE Trans. on Software Engineering 14 (1988), 1711-1730.

11. [BaP94] Bauzer Medeiros, C., and F. Pires, Databases for GIS. ACM SIGMOD Record 23 (1994), 107-115.

12. [BeG92] Becker, L., and R.H. Güting, Rule-Based Optimization and Query Processing in an Extensible Geometric Database System. ACM Transactions on Database Systems 17 (1992), 247-303.

13. [BeHF93] Becker, L., K. Hinrichs, and U. Finke, A New Algorithm for Computing Joins with Grid Files. Proc. 9th Intl. Conf. on Data Engineering, Vienna, 1993, 190-198.

14. [Beck90] Beckmann, N., H.P. Kriegel, R. Schneider, and B. Seeger, The R*-Tree: An Efficient and Robust Access Method for Points and Rectangles. Proc. ACM SIGMOD Conf. 1990, 322-331.

15. [Be75] Bentley, J.L., Multidimensional Binary Search Trees Used for Associative Searching. Communications of the ACM 18 (1975), 509-517.

16. [BeS77] Berman, R.R., and M. Stonebraker, GEO-QUEL: A System for the Manipulation and Display of Geographic Data. Computer Graphics 11 (1977), 186-191.

17. [BrKS93a] Brinkhoff, T., H.P. Kriegel, and R. Schneider, Comparison of Approximations of Complex Objects Used for Approximation-Based Query Processing in Spatial Database Systems. Proc. 9th Intl. Conf. on Data Engineering, Vienna, 1993, 40-49.

18. [BrKS93b] Brinkhoff, T., H.P. Kriegel, and B. Seeger, Efficient Processing of Spatial Joins Using R-Trees. Proc. ACM SIGMOD Conf., Washington, 1993, 237-246.

19. [Brin94] Brinkhoff, T., H.P. Kriegel, R. Schneider, and B. Seeger, Multi-Step Processing of Spatial Joins. Proc. ACM SIGMOD Conf., Minneapolis, 1994, 197-208.

20. [Buch89] Buchmann, A., O. Günther, T.R. Smith, and Y.F. Wang (eds.), Proceedings of the First Intl. Symposium on Large Spatial Databases, Santa Barbara. LNCS 409, Springer, 1989.

21. [ChF80] Chang, N.S., and K.S. Fu, A Relational Database System for Images. In: S.K. Chang and K.S. Fu (eds.), Pictorial Information Systems, Springer, 1980, 288-321.

22. [ChJL89] Chang, S.K., E. Jungert, and Y. Li, The Design of Pictorial Databases Based Upon the Theory of Symbolic Projections. Proc. First Intl. Symposium on Large Spatial Databases, Santa Barbara, 1991, 303-323.

23. [ClFO93] Clementini, E., P. Di Felice, and P. van Oosterom, A Small Set of Formal Topological Relationships Suitable for End-User Interaction. Proc. 3rd Intl. Symposium on Large Spatial Databases, Singapore, 1993, 277-295.

24. [CrMW87] Cruz, I.F., A.O. Mendelzon, and P.T. Wood, A Graphical Query Language Supporting Recursion. Proc. ACM SIGMOD Conf. 1987, 323-330.

25. [CuKR93] Cui, Z., A.G. Cohn, and D.A. Randell, Qualitative and Topological Relationships in Spatial Databases. Proc. 3rd Intl. Symposium on Large Spatial Databases, Singapore, 1993, 296-315.

26. [Davi93] David, B., L. Raynal, G. Schorter, and V. Mansart, GeO2: Why Objects in a Geographical DBMS? Proc. 3rd Intl. Symposium on Large Spatial Databases, Singapore, 1993, 264-276.

27. [Daya87] Dayal, U., F. Manola, A. Buchman, U. Chakravarthy, D. Goldhirsch, S. Heiler, J. Orenstein, and A. Rosenthal, Simplifying Complex Objects: The PROBE Approach to Modelling and Querying Them. In: H.J. Schek and G. Schlageter (eds.), Proc. BTW 87, 1987, 17-37.

28. [DrS93] Dröge, G., and H.J. Schek, Query-Adaptive Data Space Partitioning Using Variable-Size Storage Clusters. Proc. 3rd Intl. Symposium on Large Spatial Databases, Singapore, 1993, 337-356.

29. [DrSW90] Dröge, G., H.J. Schek, and A. Wolf, Erweiterbarkeit in DASDBS (Extensibility in DASDBS). Informatik Forschung und Entwicklung 5 (1990), 162-176.

30. [Eg89] Egenhofer, M., A Formal Definition of Binary Topological Relationships. Proc. 3rd Intl. Conf. on Foundations of Data Organization and Algorithms, Paris, 1989, 457-472.

31. [Eg91a] Egenhofer, M., Extending SQL for Cartographic Display. Cartography and Geographic Information Systems 18 (1991), 230-245.

32. [Eg91b] Egenhofer, M., Reasoning about Binary Topological Relations. Proc. 2nd Intl. Symposium on Large Spatial Databases, Zürich, 1991, 143-160.

33. [Eg92] Egenhofer, M., Why not SQL! Intl. Journal of Geographical Information Systems 6 (1992), 71-85.

34. [Eg94] Egenhofer, M., Spatial SQL: A Query and Presentation Language. IEEE Transactions on Knowledge and Data Engineering 6 (1994), 86-95.

35. [EgF88] Egenhofer, M., and A. Frank, Towards a Spatial Query Language: User Interface Considerations. Proc. 14th Intl. Conf. on Very Large Data Bases, Los Angeles, 1988, 124-133.

36. [EgFJ89] Egenhofer, M., A. Frank, and J.P. Jackson, A Topological Data Model for Spatial Databases. Proc. First Intl. Symposium on Large Spatial Databases, Santa Barbara, 1989, 271-286.

37. [EgH90] Egenhofer, M., and J. Herring, A Mathematical Framework for the Definition of Topological Relationships. 4th Intl. Symposium on Spatial Data Handling, Zürich, 1990, 803-813.

38. [EgH92] Egenhofer, M., and J. Herring, Categorizing Binary Topological Relationships between Regions, Lines, and Points in Geographic Databases. University of Maine, Orono, Maine, Dept. of Surveying Engineering,

39. Technical Report, 1992.

40. [ErG91] Erwig, M., and R.H. Güting, Explicit Graphs in a Functional Model for Spatial Databases. FernUniversität Hagen, Informatik-Report 110, 1991, to appear in IEEE Transactions on Knowledge and Data Engineering.

41. [FaSR87] Faloutsos, C., T. Sellis, and N. Rossopoulos, Analysis of Object-Oriented Spatial Access Methods. Proc. ACM SIGMOD Conf., San Francisco, 1987, 426-439.

42. [Fra81] Frank, A., Application of DBMS to Land Information Systems. Proc. 7th Intl. Conf. on Very Large Data Bases, Cannes, 1981, 448-453.

43. [Fra82] Frank, A., MAPQUERY: Data Base Query Language for Retrieval of Geometric Data and their Graphical Representation. Computer Graphics 16 (1982), 199-207.

44. [Fra88] Frank, A., Overlay Processing in Spatial Information Systems. Proc. 8th Intl. Symp. on Computer-Assisted Cartography (Auto-Carto 8), Baltimore, 1988, 16-31.

45. [Fra91] Frank, A., Properties of Geographic Data: Requirements for Spatial Access Methods. Proc. 2nd Intl. Symposium on Large Spatial Databases, Zürich, 1991, 225-234.

46. [Fra92] Frank, A., Qualitative Spatial Reasoning about Distances and Directions in Geographic Space. Journal of Visual Languages and Computing 3 (1992), 343-371.

47. [FraK86] Frank, A., and W. Kuhn, Cell Graphs: A Provable Correct Method for the Storage of Geometry. Proc. 2nd Intl. Symposium on Spatial Data Handling, Seattle, 1986, 411-436.

48. [Fran84] Franklin, W.R., Cartographic Errors Symptomatic of Underlying Algebra Problems. Proc. First Intl. Symposium on Spatial Data Handling, Zürich, 1984, 190-208.

49. [FrA87] Freeman, H., and J. Ahn, On the Problem of Placing Names in a Geographic Map. Intl. Journal on Pattern Recognition and Artificial Intelligence 1 (1987), 121-140.

50. [Fr87] Freeston, M.W., The BANG File: A New Kind of Grid File. Proc. ACM SIGMOD Conf., San Francisco, 260-269.

51. [Fr91] Freksa, C., Qualitative Spatial Reasoning. In: D.M. Mark and A. Frank (eds.), Cognitive and Linguistic Aspects of Geographic Space. Kluwer, Dordrecht 1991.

52. [Gard89] Gardarin, G., J.P. Cheiney, G. Kiernan, D. Pastre, and H. Stora, Managing Complex Objects in an Extensible Relational DBMS. Proc. 15th Intl. Conf. on Very Large Data Bases, Amsterdam, 1989, 55-65.

53. [GaNT91] Gargano, M., E. Nardelli, and M. Talamo, Abstract Data Types for the Logical Modeling of Complex Data. Information Systems 16, 5 (1991).

54. [Ga82] Gargantini, I., An Effective Way to Represent Quadtrees. Communications of the ACM 25 (1982), 905910.

55. [GrD87] Graefe, G., and D.J. DeWitt, The EXODUS Optimizer Generator. Proc. ACM SIGMOD 1987, 160-172.

56. [Gr89] Greene, D., An Implementation and Performance Analysis of Spatial Data Access Methods. Proc. 5th Intl. Conf. on Data Engineering, Los Angeles, 1989, 606-615.

57. [GrY86] Greene, D., and F. Yao, Finite-Resolution Computational Geometry. Proc. 27th IEEE Symp. on Foundations of Computer Science, 1986, 143-152.

58. [Gün88] Günther, O., Efficient Structures for Geometric Data Management. LNCS 337, Springer, 1988.

59. [Gün93] Günther, O., Efficient Computation of Spatial Joins. Proc. 9th Intl. Conf. on Data Engineering, Vienna, 1993, 50-59.

60. [GünB89] Günther, O., and J. Bilmes, The Implementation of the Cell Tree: Design Alternatives and Performance Evaluation. GI-Fachtagung Datenbanksysteme in Büro, Technik und Wissenschaft, Informatik-Fachberichte

61. 204, Springer, 1989, 246-265.

62. [GünB90] Günther, O., and A. Buchmann, Research Issues in Spatial Databases. ACM SIGMOD Record 19 (1990), 61-68.

63. [GünS91] Günther, O., and H.J. Schek (eds.), Proceedings of the 2nd Intl. Symposium on Large Spatial Databases, Zürich. LNCS 525, Springer, 1991.

64. [Güt88] Güting, R.H., Geo-Relational Algebra: A Model and Query Language for Geometric Database Systems. In: J.W. Schmidt, S. Ceri, M. Missikoff (eds.), Proc. EDBT 1988, 506-527.

65. [Güt89] Güting, R.H., Gral: An Extensible Relational Database System for Geometric Applications. Proc. 15th Intl. Conf. on Very Large Data Bases, Amsterdam, 1989, 33-44.

66. [Güt93] Güting, R.H., Second-Order Signature: A Tool for Specifying Data Models, Query Processing, and Optimization. Proc. ACM SIGMOD Conf., Washington, 1993, 277-286.

67. [Güt94] Güting, R.H., GraphDB: A Data Model and Query Language for Graphs in Databases. Fernuniversität Hagen, Informatik-Report 155, 1994. Short version to appear at Proc. 20th Intl. Conf. on Very Large Data Bases, Santiago, 1994.

68. [GütS87] Güting, R.H., and W. Schilling, A Practical Divide-and-Conquer Algorithm for the Rectangle Intersection Problem. Information Sciences 42 (1987), 95-112.

69. [GütS93a] Güting, R.H., and M. Schneider, Realms: A Foundation for Spatial Data Types in Database Systems. Proc. 3rd Intl. Symposium on Large Spatial Databases, Singapore, 1993, 14-35.

70. [GütS93b] Güting, R.H., and M. Schneider, Realm-Based Spatial Data Types: The ROSE Algebra. Fernuniversität Hagen, Report 141, 1993, to appear in the VLDB Journal.

71. [GütZC89] Güting, R.H., R. Zicari, and D.M. Choy, An Algebra for Structured Office Documents. ACM Transactions on Information Systems 7 (1989), 123-157.

72. [GuWJ91] Gupta, A., T. Weymouth, and R. Jain, Semantic Queries with Pictures: The VIMSYS Model. Proc. 17th Intl. Conf. on Very Large Data Bases, Barcelona, 1991, 69-79.

73. [Gu84] Guttmann, R., R-Trees: A Dynamic Index Structure for Spatial Searching. Proc. ACM SIGMOD Conf., 1984, 47-57.

74. [GyPV90] Gyssens, M., J. Paredaens, and D. van Gucht, A Graph-Oriented Object Database Model. Proc. ACM Conf. on Principles of Database Systems 1990, 417-424.

75. [Haas89] Haas, L.M., J.C. Freytag, G.M. Lohman, and H. Pirahesh, Extensible Query Processing in Starburst. Proc. ACM SIGMOD 1989, 377-388.

76. [HaC91] Haas, L.M., and W.F. Cody, Exploiting Extensible DBMS in Integrated Geographic Information Systems. Proc. 2nd Intl. Symposium on Large Spatial Databases, Zürich, 1991, 423-450.

77. [HeSW89] Henrich, A., H.-W. Six, and P. Widmayer, The LSD-Tree: Spatial Access to Multidimensional Point- and Non-Point-Objects. Proc. 15th Intl. Conf. on Very Large Data Bases, Amsterdam, 1989, 45-53.

78. [HeLS88] Herring, J., R. Larsen, and J. Shivakumar, Extensions to the SQL Language to Support Spatial Analysis in a Topological Data Base. Proc. GIS/LIS 1988.

79. [Hi85] Hinrichs, K., The Grid File System: Implementation and Case Studies of Applications. Doctoral Thesis, ETH Zürich, 1985.

80. [HoO92] de Hoop, S., and P. van Oosterom, Storage and Manipulation of Topology in Postgres. Proc. 3rd European Conf. on Geographical Information Systems, Munich, 1992, 1324-1336.

81. [JoC88] Joseph, T., and A. Cardenas, PICQUERY: A High Level Query Language for Pictorial Database Management. IEEE Trans. on Software Engineering 14 (1988), 630-638.

82. [KePI87] Keating, T., W. Phillips, and K. Ingram, An Integrated Topologic Database Design for Geographic Information Systems. Photogrammetric Engineering & Remote Sensing 53 (1987), 1399-1402.

83. [KrHS91] Kriegel, H.P., H. Horn, and M. Schiwietz, The Performance of Object Decomposition Techniques for Spatial Query Processing. Proc. 2nd Intl. Symp. on Large Spatial Databases, Zürich, 1991, 257-276.

84. [LaPV93] Larue, T., D. Pastre, and Y. Viémont, Strong Integration of Spatial Domains and Operators in a Relational Database System. Proc. 3rd Intl. Symposium on Large Spatial Databases, Singapore, 1993, 53-72.

85. [LiN87] Lipeck, U., and K. Neumann, Modelling and Manipulating Objects in Geoscientific Databases. Proc. 5th Intl. Conf on the Entity-Relationship Approach (Dijon, 1986), 1987, 67-86.

86. [LoR94] Lo, M.L., and C.V. Ravishankar, Spatial Joins Using Seeded Trees. Proc. ACM SIGMOD Conf., Minneapolis, 1994, 209-220.

87. [LoS89] Lomet, D.B., and B. Salzberg, A Robust Multi-Attribute Search Structure. Proc. 5th Intl. Conf. on Data Engineering, Los Angeles, 1989, 296-304.

88. [LuH92] Lu, W., and J. Han, Distance-Associated Join Indices for Spatial Range Search. Proc. 9th Intl. Conf. on Data Engineering, Vienna, 1992, 284-292.

89. [MaP90] Maingenaud, M., and M. Portier, Cigales: A Graphical Query Language for Geographical Information Systems. Proc. 4th Intl. Symposium on Spatial Data Handling, Zürich, 1990, 393-404.

90. [MaC80] Mantey, P.E., and E.D. Carlson, Integrated Geographic Data Bases: The GADS Experience. In: A. Blaser (ed.), Data Base Techniques for Pictorial Applications, Springer, 1980, 173-198.

91. [Me84] Mehlhorn, K., Data Structures and Algorithms 3: Multi-dimensional Searching and Computational Geometry. Springer, 1984.

92. [Me92] Meyer, B., Beyond Icons: Towards New Metaphors for Visual Query Languages for Spatial Information Systems. In: R. Cooper (ed.), Interfaces to Database Systems, Springer, 1992, 113-135.

93. [Mo89] Morehouse, S., The Architecture of ARC/INFO. Proc. Auto-Carto 9, Baltimore, 1989.

94. [Mo66] Morton, G.M., A Computer Oriented Geodetic Data Base and a New Technique in File Sequencing. IBM, Ottawa, Canada, 1966.

95. [NiHS84] Nievergelt, J., H. Hinterberger, and K.C. Sevcik, The Grid File: An Adaptable, Symmetric Multikey File Structure. ACM Transactions on Database Systems 9 (1984), 38-71. [NiP82] Nievergelt, J., and F.P. Preparata, Plane-Sweep Algorithms for Intersecting Geometric Figures. Communications of the ACM 25 (1982), 739-747.

96. [OoMS87] Ooi, B.C., K.J. McDonell, and R. Sacks-Davis, Spatial kd-Tee: An Indexing Mechanism for Spatial Databases. Proc. IEEE COMPSAC Conf., Tokyo, 1987, 433-438.

97. [OoSM89] Ooi, B.C., R. Sacks-Davis, and K.J. McDonell, Extending a DBMS for Geographic Applications. Proc. 5th Intl. Conf. on Data Engineering, Los Angeles, 1989, 590-597.

98. [OoV91] van Oosterom, P., and T. Vijlbrief, Building a GIS on Top of the Open DBMS POSTGRES. Proc. 2nd European Conf. on Geographical Informations Systems (EGIS 91), Brussels, 1991, 775-787.

99. [Or86] Orenstein, J.A., Spatial Query Processing in an Object-Oriented Database System. Proc. ACM SIGMOD Conf. 1986, 326-336.

100.   [Or89] Orenstein, J.A., Strategies for Optimizing the Use of Redundancy in Spatial Databases. Proc. First Intl. Symposium on Large Spatial Databases, Santa Barbara, 1989, 115-134.

101.   [Or91] Orenstein, J.A., An Algorithm for Computing the Overlay of k-Dimensional Spaces. Proc. 2nd Intl. Symposium on Large Spatial Databases, Zürich, 1991, 381-400.

102.   [OrM88] Orenstein, J., and F. Manola, PROBE Spatial Data Modeling and Query Processing in an Image Database Application. IEEE Trans. on Software Engineering 14 (1988), 611-629.

103.   [OsH86] Osborn, S.L., and T.E. Heaven, The Design of a Relational Database System with Abstract Data Types for Domains. ACM Transactions on Database Systems 11 (1986), 357-373.

104.   [PaST93] Pagel, B.U., H.W. Six, and H. Toben, The Transformation Technique for Spatial Objects Revisited. Proc. 3rd Intl. Symposium on Large Spatial Databases, Singapore, 1993, 73-88.

105.   [PrS85] Preparata, F.P., and M.I. Shamos, Computational Geometry: An Introduction. Springer 1985.

106.   [PuE88] Pullar, D., and M. Egenhofer, Towards Formal Definitions of Topological Relations Among Spatial Objects. Proc. 3rd Intl. Symposium on Spatial Data Handling, Sydney, 1988, 225-242.

107.   [Ri94] de Ridder, T., Die ROSE-Algebra: Implementierung geometrischer Datentypen und Operationen für erweiterbare Datenbanksysteme (The ROSE Algebra: Implementation of Geometric Data Types and Operations for Extensible Database Systems). Fernuniversität Hagen, Fachbereich Informatik, Diplomarbeit (Master Thesis), 1994.

108.   [Ro81] Robinson, J.T., The KDB-Tree: A Search Structure for Large Multidimensional Dynamic Indexes. Proc. ACM SIGMOD Conf., 1981, 10-18.

109.   [Rose86] Rosenthal, A., S. Heiler, U. Dayal, and F. Manola, Traversal Recursion: A Practical Approach to Supporting Recursive Applications. Proc. ACM SIGMOD Conf. 1986, 166-176.

110.   [RoFS88] Rossopoulos, N., C. Faloutsos, and T. Sellis, An Efficient Pictorial Database System for PSQL. IEEE Trans. on Software Engineering 14 (1988), 639-650.

111.   [Ro91] Rotem, D., Spatial Join Indices. Proc. 7th Intl. Conf. on Data Engineering, Kobe, Japan, 1991, 500-509.

112.   [Sa90] Samet, H., The Design and Analysis of Spatial Data Structures. Addison-Wesley, 1990.

113.   [Sche90] Schek, H.J., H.B. Paul, M.H. Scholl, and G. Weikum, The DASDBS Project: Objectives, Experiences, and Future Prospects. IEEE Transactions on Knowledge and Data Engineering 2 (1990), 25-43.

114.   [ScW93] Schek, H.J., and A. Wolf, From Extensible Databases to Interoperability between Multiple Databases and GIS Applications. Proc. 3rd Intl. Symposium on Large Spatial Databases, Singapore, 1993, 207-238.

115.   [Sc85] Schilcher, M., Interactive Graphic Data Processing in Cartography. Computers & Graphics 9 (1985), 5766.

116.   [ScV89] Scholl, M., and A. Voisard, Thematic Map Modeling. Proc. First Intl. Symp. on Large Spatial Databases, Santa Barbara, 1989, 167-190.

117.   [ScV92] Scholl, M., and A. Voisard, Object-Oriented Database Systems for Geographic Applications: An Experiment with O2. In: G. Gambosi, H. Six, and M.

Scholl (eds.) Proc. Int. Workshop on Database Management Systems for Geographical Applications, (Capri, 1991), Springer, 1992, 103-137.

118.   [SeK88] Seeger, B., and H.P. Kriegel, Techniques for Design and Implementation of Efficient Spatial Access Methods. Proc. 14th Intl. Conf on Very Larga Data Bases, Los Angeles, 1988, 360-371.

119.   [SeK90] Seeger, B., and H.P. Kriegel, The Buddy-Tree: An Efficient and Robust Access Method for Spatial Database Systems. Proc. 16th Intl. Conf. on Very Large Data Bases, Brisbane, Australia, 1990, 590-601.

120.   [SeRF87] Sellis, T., N. Rossopoulos, and C. Faloutsos, The R+-Tree: A Dynamic Index for Multi-Dimensional Objects. Proc. 13th Intl. Conf. on Very Large Data Bases, Brighton, 1987, 507-518.

121.   [SmG90] Smith, T.R., and P. Gao, Experimental Performance Evaluations on Spatial Access Methods. Proc. 4th Intl. Symposium on Spatial Data Handling, Zürich, 1990, 991-1002.

122.   [Smit87] Smith, T.R., S. Menon, J.L. Star, and J.E. Estes, Requirements and Principles for the Implementation and Construction of Large-Scale Geographic Information Systems. Intl. Journal of Geographical Information Systems 1 (1987), 13-31.

123.   [Ston93] Stonebraker, M., J. Frew, K. Gardels, and J. Meredith, The Sequoia 2000 Storage Benchmark. Proc. ACM SIGMOD Conf., Washington, 1993, 2-11.

124.   [StFD93] Stonebraker, M., J. Frew, and J. Dozier, The SEQUOIA 2000 Project. Proc. 3rd Intl. Symposium on Large Spatial Databases, Singapore, 1993, 397-412.

125.   [StR86] Stonebraker, M., and L.A. Rowe, The Design of POSTGRES. Proc. of the 1986 SIGMOD Conf. (Washington, DC, May 1986), 340-355.

126.   [StRG83] Stonebraker, M., B. Rubenstein, and A. Guttmann, Application of Abstract Data Types and Abstract Indices to CAD Databases. Proc. ACM Engineering Design Applications Conf., 1983, 107-114.

127.   [SvH91] Svensson, P., and Z. Huang, Geo-SAL: A Query Language for Spatial Data Analysis. Proc. 2nd Intl. Symposium on Large Spatial Databases, Zürich, 1991, 119-140.

128.   [Ta82] Tamminen, M., The Extendible Cell Method for Closest Point Problems. BIT 22 (1982), 27-41.

129.   [To90] Tomlin, C.D., Geographic Information Systems and Cartographic Modeling. Prentice Hall, 1990.

130.   [Va87] Valduriez, P., Join Indices. ACM Transactions on Database Systems 12 (1987), 218-246.

131.   [ViO92] Vijlbrief, T., and P. van Oosterom, The GEO++ System: An Extensible GIS. Proc. 5th Intl. Symposium on Spatial Data Handling, Charleston, South Carolina, 1992, 40-50.

132.   [Vo91] Voisard, A., Towards a Toolbox for Geographic User Interfaces. Proc. 2nd Intl. Symposium on Large Spatial Databases, Zürich, 1991, 75-97.

133.   [WaH87] Waugh, T.C., and R.G. Healey. The GEOVIEW Design: A Relational Data Base Approach to Geographical Data Handling. Intl. Journal of Geographical Information Systems 1 (1987), 101-118.

134.   [Wi91] Widmayer, P., Datenstrukturen für Geodatenbanken (Data Structures for Spatial Databases). In: G. Vossen (ed.), Entwicklungstendenzen bei Datenbanksystemen. Oldenbourg, München, 1991, 317-361.

135.   [Wilm88] Wilms, P.F., P.M. Schwarz, H.-J. Schek, and L.M. Haas, Incorporating Data Types in an Extensible Database Architecture. Proc. 3rd Intl. Conf. on Data and Knowledge Bases, Jerusalem, 1988, 180-192.

136.   [Wo89] Wolf, A., The DASDBS GEO-Kernel: Concepts, Experiences, and the Second Step. Proc. First Intl. Symposium on Large Spatial Databases, Santa Barbara, 1989, 67-88.

137.   [Wo92] Worboys, M.F., A Generic Model for Planar Geographical Objects. Intl. Journal of Geographical Information Systems (1992), 353-372.

138.   Mark Monmonier How to Lie with Maps University of Chicago Press, 1996.

139.   De Knegt; H.J.; F. van Langevelde; M.B. Coughenour; A.K. Skidmore; W.F. de Boer; I.M.A. Heitkönig; N.M. Knox; R. Slotow; C. van der Waal and H.H.T. Prins (2010). Spatial autocorrelation and the scaling of species–environment relationships. Ecology 91: 2455–2465. doi:10.1890/09-1359.1

140.   Graham J. Upton & Bernard Fingelton: Spatial Data Analysis by Example Volume 1: Point Pattern and Quantitative Data John Wiley & Sons, New York. 1985.

141.   Honarkhah, M and Caers, J, 2010, Stochastic Simulation of Patterns Using Distance-Based Pattern Modeling, Mathematical Geosciences, 42: 487 – 517

142.   N. Adam and A. Gangopadhyay, Database Issues in Geographical Information Systems, Kluwer, 1997.

143.   T. Asano, D. Ranjan, T. Roos, E. Wiezl, and P. Widmayer, "Space Filling Curves and Their Use In The Design of Geometric Data   Structures," Theoretical Computer Science, vol. 181, no. 1, pp. 3–15, July 1996.

144.   P. Baumann, "Management of Multidimensional Discrete Data," VLDB J., special issue on spatial database systems, vol. 3, no. 4, pp. 401–444, Oct. 1994.

145.   A. Belussi and C. Faloutsos, "Estimating the Selectivity of Spatial Queries Using the 'Correlation' Fractal Dimension," Proc. 21st Int'l Conf. Very Large Data Bases, pp. 299–310, Zurich, Sept. 1995.

146.   T. Brinkhoff, H.-P. Kriegel, and B. Seeger, "Efficient Processing of Spatial Joins Using R-Trees," Proc. SIGMOD Conf. Management of Data, pp. 237–246, Washington D.C., ACM, June 1993.

147.   D. Chamberlin, Using The New DB2: IBM's Object Relational System, Morgan Kaufmann, 1997.

148.   N. Chrisman, Exploring Geographic Information Systems, John Wiley and Sons, 1997.

149.   E. Clemintini and P. Di Felice, "Topological Invariants for Lines," IEEE Trans. Knowledge and Data Eng., vol. 10, no. 1, pp. 38–54, 1998

150.   D.J. DeWitt, N. Kabra, J. Luo, J.M. Patel, and J.-B. Yu, "ClientServer Paradise," Proc. 20th Int'l Conf. Very Large Data Bases, pp. 558–569, Santiago de Chile, Chile, Sept. 1994.

151.   M. Egenhofer, "Spatial SQL: A Query and Presentation Language," IEEE Trans. Knowledge and Data Eng., vol. 6, no. 1, pp. 86–95, 1994.

152.   R.H. Güting, "An Introduction to Spatial Database Systems," VLDB J., special issue on spatial database systems, vol. 3, no. 4, pp. 357–399, 1994.

153.   R. Guttman, "R-Tree: A Dynamic Index Structure for Spatial Searching," Proc. SIGMOD Conf., Ann. Meeting, pp. 47–57, Boston, ACM, 1984.

154.   J.M. Hellerstein and M. Stonebraker, "Predicate Migration: Optimizing Queries with Expensive Predicates," Proc. SIGMOD Int'l Conf. Management of Data, pp. 267–276, Washington, D.C., ACM,May 1993.

155.   N. Jing, Y. Huang, and E. Rundensteiner, "Hierarchical Encoded Path Views for Path Query Processing: An Optimal Model and Its Performance Evaluation," IEEE Trans. Knowledge and Data Eng., vol. 10, no. 3, pp. 409–432, 1998.

156.   W. Kim, J. Garza, and A. Kesin, "Spatial Data Management in Database Systems," Proc. Third Int'l Symp Advances in Spatial Databases, pp.1–13, Lecture notes in Computer Science 692, SpringerVerlag, Singapore, 1993.

157.   M. Kornacker and D. Banks, "High-Concurrency Locking in R-Trees," Proc. 21st Int'l Conf. Very Large Data Bases, pp. 134–145, Zurich, Sept. 1995.

158.   R. Laurini and D. Thompson, Fundamentals of Spatial Information Systems, Academic Press, 1992.

159.   J. Lee, Y. Lee, K. Whang, and I. Song, "A Physical Database Design Method for Multidimensional File Organization," Information Sciences, vol. 120, no. 1, pp. 31–65, Oct. 1997.

160.   Y. Theodoridis, E. Stefanakis, and T. Sellis, "Cost Models for Join Queries in Spatial Databases," Proc. 14th Int'l Conf. Data Eng., pp. 476–483, Orlando, Fla., Feb. 1998